Praise for Provoking Greatness

"A generous book about stepping up to make art, to matter, and to contribute."
—Seth Godin, author of What to Do When It's Your Turn

"Finally! Someone has incorporated the power of provocation into the art of leadership!"
—Nido Qubein, president, High Point University

"Reading this book is like flipping the 'on' switch to your own potential and that of your team. Greatness is an inside job. You don't have to go out and get anything; it's already in you and the people in your organization. This book will show you how to provoke it."
—Joe Callaway, author of Be the Best at What Matters Most

"If you want to live—and lead—with intention, this is the textbook on how to become great!"
—Randy Gage, author of the New York Times bestseller, *Risky Is the New Safe*

"With the eloquently brisk prose and memorable anecdotes for which Misti Burmeister is known, Provoking Greatness will awaken your intellect with practical and meaningful insight that can make your organization soar. From the moment you discover how internal vulnerability can be the impetus for propelling those you mentor or influence to higher effectiveness in their personal and business lives, I think you will be as captivated as I was. Burmeister delivers clear, helpful guidance based on her highly acclaimed business consulting experience, and enhanced with solid research and pithy examples of contemporary business leaders. Provocation is a challenge and a gift."
—Tim Overstreet, associate dean, U.S. Army Logistics University

"*Finding your true voice—your point of view—is said to be worth 10,000 I.Q. points. Misti's book helps you find that voice and then gives you the steps to express it.*"

—Verne Harnish, founder, Entrepreneurs' Organization; CEO, Gazelles; author of *Scaling Up*

"*This book dispels myths about motivation and provides the right amount of insight and guidance for budding leaders and executives alike. I learned the art of provoking greatness and have already starting seeing results. Get this book!*"

—Janie Tiedeman., transportation engineer

"*Provoking Greatness is a rarity—a great book for recent college grads and for 30-year CEOs. Misti's years of research, refreshing perspective, and unique ideas have been transformed into actionable tasks to help you achieve your professional goals. Read this book to improve yourself, your team, and your general satisfaction at work.*"

—Mike Lombardi, board member, Baltimore Angels

PROVOKING GREATNESS

Unleashing Hidden Potentials

Misti Burmeister

Synergy Press
www.synergypressonline.com

Book Layout by Unauthorized Media, LLC

For details, contact Special Markets Department, Synergy Press, LLC at info@synergypressonline.com.

Provoking Greatness : Unleashing Hidden Potential / Misit Burmeister —1st ed.

ISBN 13: 978-0-9802209-7-1

For Worldwide Distribution, Printed in the U.S.A.

Table of Contents

SECTION 4: COMMUNITY

SECTION 5: ENERGY

Dedication

This book is dedicated to Mrs. Taylor Mallory Holland, my editor. Your gentle, kind approach has been a guiding light through some of the darkest times in my life. Thank you!

Why Provoke?

"There are leaders, and then there are those who lead. Leaders hold a position of power or authority. But those who lead inspire us. Whether they're individuals or organizations, we follow those who lead, not because we have to, but because we want to. We follow, not for them, but for ourselves."

—*Simon Sinek*

What wakes people up to the greatness that exists inside of them? What is it that leaves people wanting to see beyond self-imposed limitations and achieve something meaningful, even remarkable? What creates the spark that pushes people into caring about their results? And how can you provoke—and harness—all that greatness in your team?

These are the guiding questions behind this book. Whether you're an entrepreneur, a seasoned executive, a mid-level manager, or just starting out on your leadership journey, provoking greatness begins with recognizing the greatness that exists inside of you.

Attracting and retaining good people with positive energy requires more than a fancy title and the promise of a paycheck. It requires leaders with VOICE, who are capable of not only seeing the greatness in others, but also provoking it.

A Long History of Provoking

While the word *provoke* often has negative connotations—as in to provoke anger or an argument—positive feelings and events can be provoked just as easily as negative ones. My own life has been shaped by plenty of provokers—some of them helpful and some hazardous.

Whether it's for better or for worse, being provoked isn't comfortable. Most of us want to grow into our potential, but the change, learning, and vulnerability that come with the process don't always feel good or safe. Provoking greatness requires a lot of hard "heart" work, and it's also the best thing you can do for yourself and others.

Everyone has greatness inside of them; most of us just need a little help seeing it. That's why, whether we know it or not, we flock to leaders who can help us discover our natural talents and guide us to challenges that will ultimately put those talents to good use.

In fact, I was provoked into writing this book by a coach named Greg Conderacci in Baltimore, Maryland, who has a special gift for helping others identify and communicate their purpose. I'd enlisted his support because I knew it was time for my message to evolve. The generational diversity consulting that launched my coaching career and first book—*From Boomers to Bloggers*—was still important to me, but I knew I had more to share. I simply couldn't put my finger on how to package my new message.

In preparation for my third meeting with Greg, I pinned up giant Post-it notes on the walls and outlined the flow of my next speech, complete with stories and points to draw from each anecdote. As I talked him through it, he stopped me when I got to "Ms. Cays"—a story I often tell about the high-school English teacher who unknowingly provoked my greatness.

Ms. Cays was not my favorite teacher. She had all kinds of rules, and I was a teenager with raging hormones, a bad case of laziness, and a talkative nature that drove my teachers nuts. One day I walked into her classroom, late and without the essay I was supposed to turn in. My tardiness and missing homework weren't the least bit unusual, but her response on this day was.

When Ms. Cays asked me to see her after class, I knew I'd earned myself another detention slip. Instead she just looked at me and said, "If I took a wire, inserted it into your mouth, and ran it down your arms to your fingertips, we'd have a writer on our hands." Then she turned and walked out the door.

"A writer was born that day," I told Greg. "No, I didn't begin furiously writing that day, but I did write my next paper. The seed was planted, and 10 years later, I had a bestselling book."

"Misti," Greg jumped in, suddenly excited. "Teach me how to do *that,* how to get people to use their natural talents…*on purpose.* It's done unintentionally all the time, but certainly there's a science behind it. Go figure it out and teach it to me."

The VOICE Model

With a keen interest in discovering the *secret* formula for provoking greatness, I spent the next couple years researching the science behind motivation and studying provocative leaders to learn what they do differently.

While I did not discover a magical formula, I did find five commonalities among those who masterfully provoke greatness in others:

V	Vision	Painting a clear picture of an ideal future that inspires people into action
O	Ownership	Accepting full responsibility for results
I	Intentions	Being purposeful about intended outcomes
C	Community	Fostering environments where people feel connected to one another
E	Energy	Having passion and unstoppable drive at the highest level within a company

VOICE is the perfect analogy to reflect what's needed to provoke greatness. You must trust and use your voice to take a stand for greatness. If you don't trust your voice—if you don't believe in what you are provoking—you will fail. If Ms. Cays hadn't seen my potential, she would not have provoked my greatness. If I had thought she was trying to manipulate me into doing my homework, or to get me to do something for *her* good, she would not have provoked my greatness. Ultimately I believed she meant what she said...what she *voiced*.

I have yet to interview a single successful person—and I've interviewed hundreds (dozens for this book alone)—who got where they are without the support and encouragement of others. Each of them shared stories about people who saw something in them they could not see at the time...and then VOICED it. As a result, these provokers gave them a new *vision* of what was possible for their lives.

This book is for leaders at all levels who want to make *that* kind of difference in the lives of the people they lead. It is for those who are tired of pushing people to perform and would rather create an environment where people *want* to give their best. No one is perfect in every area of the VOICE model, but in this book, you will learn how to systematically increase your effectiveness in each.

There's No VOICE Without Vulnerability

First, a word of warning: None of the strategies in these pages will work if you're only leading with your head. VOICE-inspired leadership also requires heart.

Most leaders would rather simply pay employees to push *themselves* to peak performance. But few people can do that. Just like world-class athletes have coaches, world-class employees need leaders willing and able to provoke them, and to challenge them with meaningful work.

A paycheck is enough to find someone who will put in the bare minimum, but attracting good people with positive energy requires more than a clearly-defined understanding of your product, market, and competitive advantages. It requires a *deep understanding of people*—what inspires them, what excites them, and what they need to be successful.

It's emotional stuff, but it's not weak or soft. It's powerful and radical, and it produces hardcore bottom-line results.

There's plenty of research making the business case for emotional intelligence, much of which I will share throughout this book. Yet far too many leaders ignore its importance. Why? Because it requires vulnerability, which can be uncomfortable—especially in the work environment, where there's a prevailing misperception you're supposed to know everything and be perfect. It is through our imperfections and mistakes that we learn, grow, create, and add value. And it is through vulnerability that we connect with others.

This idea is at the heart of Brené Brown's groundbreaking work. Her Ted Talk, "The Power of Vulnerability," has received more than 16 million views and has been translated into more than 48 languages—all because she has tapped into a particularly powerful truth: People are starved for connection, and they flock to companies, leaders, visions, and missions that help them feel connected to others.

In her book, *Daring Greatly,* Brown makes the connection between successful leadership and vulnerability: "If we want to reignite innovation and passion, we have to rehumanize work. When shame becomes a management style, engagement dies. When failure is not an option, we can forget about learning, creativity, and innovation."[1]

Vulnerability is powerful, and yet it is the very thing that scares many leaders away from being provocative leaders. It's uncomfortable, unfamiliar territory, so they ignore all evidence that "soft skills" matter just as much—if not more— than what's taught in business schools. Numbers and business systems are easy; dealing with emotions is the hard stuff. It's also the key to provoking greatness.

Vulnerability Required Beyond This Point
Vulnerability permeates the entire VOICE model. Holding a vision

---

1 Brené Brown. *Daring Greatly: How the Courage to Be Vulnerable Transforms the Way We Live, Love, Parent, and Lead.* Gotham, 2012.

for a new or better future brings with it the possibility of failure. Being transparent about our intentions insists on vulnerability, as does taking ownership of our results (knowing we might be judged poorly if we fall short). At the core of community is authentic connection, which requires (yep, you got it) *vulnerability*. And having enough energy to push your team to the finish line means admitting you're not perfect and that you need support, which sounds pretty vulnerable to me.

Throughout this book, I will share hard numbers, scientific research, and real-life success stories that demonstrate the effectiveness of the VOICE model. I will also share actionable steps to help you cultivate your own VOICE.

So are you ready to wake up to the greatness that exists inside of you? How about that of those surrounding you every day?

Section 1: Vision

Vision: Painting a clear picture of an ideal future that inspires people into action

Leaders who establish compelling visions for their teams don't have to worry about motivating people to do great work. When a team knows where it's headed, why it's important to get there, and how each person contributes to making the vision a reality, it remains inspired and focused throughout the long, rewarding journey.

When I interviewed Rich Fairbank, CEO and founder of Capital One, he told me about the visionary leaders who inspire him. "These leaders are fanatical," he explained. "They are on a quest to achieve something extraordinary, and nothing will get in their way."

The energy inherent in those words struck a chord in me. The concept of a "quest" is the perfect way to think about vision. A powerful vision is an outcome so inspiring that those involved in bringing it to fruition will journey to the ends of the earth to make it happen.

Yet despite all the evidence and arguments for the value of vision, only 3 percent of the typical business leader's time is spent envisioning and enlisting others in his vision.[2]

If motivation really is this simple, why don't more leaders tap into the inexhaustible inspiration created by such visions? Why

---

2 James M. Kouzes and Barry Z. Posner. "To Lead, Create a Shared Vision," *Harvard Business Review*. Jan. 2009. <http://hbr.org/2009/01/to-lead-create-a-shared-vision/ar/1>.

is "visionary" a title reserved for only a few, especially when there are countless books and articles detailing the importance of vision?

The short answer is that getting clarity around one's vision takes time. Many leaders think they need to spend their days putting out fires, creating business plans, and focusing on the bottom line. They don't make time for envisioning the future or sharing their passion.

Leaders and companies who *do* prioritize vision get remarkable results. While conducting research for *Built to Last: Successful Habits of Visionary Companies*, authors James C. Collins and Jerry I. Porras found that "visionary companies" have outperformed the general stock market by a factor of 12 since 1925. They summarize:

> **"** Truly great companies understand the difference between what should never change and what should be open for change, between what is genuinely sacred and what is not. This rare ability to manage continuity and change—requiring a consciously practiced discipline—is closely linked to the ability to develop a vision. Vision provides guidance about what core to preserve and what future to stimulate progress toward. But vision has become one of the most overused and least understood words in the language.[3]

To provoke greatness, you must quiet the noise long enough to contemplate where your ship is headed and why it's important to reach that destination.

In this section, we'll discuss three different but equally important types of vision:

1. The company's overall vision, as created by the entrepreneur or executive team

2. An individual leader's vision for his or her team, which is

---

3 James M. Kouzes and Barry Z. Posner. "To Lead, Create a Shared Vision," *Harvard Business Review*. Jan. 2009. <http://hbr.org/2009/01/to-lead-create-a-shared-vision/ar/1>.

not necessarily the same as the company's overall vision but should be aligned with it

3. A leader's vision for—or beliefs about—the people on his or her team

Using these distinctions to guide the conversation, let's dive into the value of vision, how to create a vision that inspires and drives your team to achieve it, and what might be getting in the way of bringing your vision to life.

CHAPTER 1

20/20 Vision: How Important Is It?

"If there is one door in the castle you have been told not to go through, you must. Otherwise, you'll just be rearranging furniture in rooms you've already been in."

— Anne Lamott

There's a good reason Steve Jobs didn't define his vision for Apple as: "To become the No. 1 computer company in the world." That might have been part of his intended outcome, but it's not what moved his people into greatness. On the other hand, to have "1,000 songs in my pocket" did provoke greatness—in both Jobs and his team, enabling them to revolutionize the music industry.[4]

The same goes for Jeff Bezos—founder of Amazon, owner of *The Washington Post*, and the 19th richest man in the world. He set a clear, forward-thinking, achievable vision for both Amazon—"to be Earth's most customer-centric company, where shoppers everywhere can discover anything they might want to buy online"[5]—and then for the Kindle—to make "every book ever printed in any language all available in less than 60 seconds."[6] Today Amazon is the world's largest online retailer, and Kindle has become a household name.

Vishen Lakhiani, founder of online publishing company Mindvalley, has created such a loud buzz that people move to Malaysia just to be part of his vision. Lakhiani started his company while living in New York, having left his home country of Malaysia. At that time, Malaysia had very few opportunities for highly-edu-

---

4 Steve Jobs. "Original iPod 1000 Songs in your pocket by Steve Jobs" [video file]. YouTube.com, Sep. 21, 2011. <https://www.youtube.com/watch?feature=player_embedded&v=6SUJNspeux8>.
5 "Company Facts," Amazon Press Room. Retrieved Nov. 2, 2014. <http://phx.corporate-ir.net/phoenix.zhtml?c=176060&p=irol-factSheet>.
6 "EX-99.1 2 dex991.htm 2008 LETTER TO SHAREHOLDERS," *SEC.gov*. Retrieved Nov. 2, 2014. <http://www.sec.gov/Archives/edgar/data/1018724/000119312509081096/dex991.htm>.

cated, driven people, so many of the country's best and brightest left in search of a better future. But when Lakhiani's visa expired, and he was forced to return home, he set a new vision: to create a company culture that would attract talented, well-educated people from all over the world to Malaysia.[7]

His plan worked, and today Mindvalley is revolutionizing the education industry. It has been named one of *Inc.* magazine's "Top 10 World's Coolest Offices" and won WorldBlu's global "Most Democratic Workplace Award" five years in a row.[8] Not only has the company's revenue soared, but Mindvalley is well on its way to achieving Lakhiani's latest vision: to make "the world a better place by touching 1 billion lives by the year 2050."

Vision is exceptionally valuable, but only if it inspires and provokes the people working to achieve it. Your vision must be a powerful call to action—an invitation to join your quest—and not just some verbiage to put in the company handbook.

Think Bigger

It's not enough to say you want to become the best, most profitable company. Every company wants to be No. 1 and to make the most money. Your vision needs to tap into something much greater than money—or as Capital One CEO Rich Fairbank put it, *something bigger* than you.

Here's what he told me:

> ❝ The real difference in life is whether you're chasing your own greatness or chasing something that's great. So many of the people who have a quest are trying to pursue their own advancement, and they have great passion too. But from a leadership point of view, it's really hard to get people to follow that. Imagine going home at night and saying, "Honey, I am going to have to stay up all night working so my boss can get his promotion." I mean, that's not a quest that other people

7 Vishen Lakhiani. "5 Steps to Creating the World's Greatest Workplace (Ted Talk)" [video file]. YouTube.com, Feb. 6, 2012. <http://www.youtube.com/watch?v=l22XuUFWoCI>.
8 "How it Started." Mindvalley. <http://www.mindvalley.com/about>.

want to follow. In contrast, leaders who chase a quest that's bigger than they are, are often very successful, but success is a byproduct, not the objective function.

A compelling vision—one powerful enough to spark your passion, inspire your team, and keep everyone motivated when success seems impossible—captures exactly what you hope you achieve, why you want to achieve it, and *when* you want to achieve it. It is specific, measurable, and often has a date associated with it. It is clear, compelling, and consistently communicated. Most importantly, it inspires and engages everyone involved—the visionary, the team, and the community at large.

President Kennedy *didn't* say he wanted the U.S. "to become the No. 1 shuttle designer in the world." His quest was "landing a man on the moon and returning him safely to the earth" by the end of the decade.[9] As a result of this very specific vision, and his clarity about what was at stake if the vision was not achieved, our country reached the moon eight years later.

Likewise, Southwest Airlines didn't just aim to sell more plane tickets than anyone else. The vision was to make air travel accessible to the average person.[10] When the company started out in the '70s, only 15 percent of Americans had ever flown. Now more than 85 percent have experienced air travel, in part due to Southwest's vision and efforts to make flying more affordable for all Americans.

Think Improbable, but Not Impossible

A strong vision aims high but is also achievable, which means you might have to set a new vision once you've succeeded in bringing the first one to life. Jobs and his team achieved their vision, and then reset—turning a product capable of holding 1,000 songs in your pocket into a device that does so much more. Imagine if NASA had stopped envisioning after reaching the moon. We certainly wouldn't have a monster truck roving around on Mars right

---

9 Jennifer Rosenberg. "President John F. Kennedy's Man on the Moon Speech," *About.com Education*. <http://history1900s.about.com/od/1960s/a/jfkmoon.htm>.
10 Simon Sinek. *Start with Why: How Great Leaders Inspire Everyone to Take Action*. Portfolio Trade, 2011.

now, collecting valuable information to help us better understand our planet and solar system.

To be fair, some visions are so big that their creators don't live long enough to see them completed. Consider, for example, the beautiful European churches built centuries ago—one etching at a time, one brick at a time, and one moment at a time. The original visionaries often died long before their masterpieces were complete. But the clarity of their visions compelled thousands of people to spend decades working toward achieving them. Today these buildings serve as exquisite places of worship and important pieces of architectural history.

Many other remarkable visionaries never got to see their dreams come to fruition, including Martin Luther King, Jr., Mother Teresa, and Mahatma Gandhi. Yet our world is a better place because they were brave enough to dream big, to set goals that were just this side of impossible, and to enroll others in bringing those visions to life.

If there's one common lesson we can learn from each of these provokers, it's that *changing the world begins and ends with changing yourself.* A quote often attributed to Gandhi: "Be the change you wish to see in the world."

This is not to say that being a powerful visionary means you must save thousands of lives, feed homeless people around the world, or usher in a civil rights movement. Many small visions have made a big difference in the communities they serve.

Marc Ecko says smaller visions can be more effective. He writes:

> ❝❝ Visions *should* start small. They're incremental, like building Legos:
>
> Snap one block to the next.
> Snap another block.
> Repeat.
>
> Having an overly majestic "vision" can cripple you with pressure. When I started with graffiti, I thought about my next 18 hours, not my next 18 years. Free yourself to do the same.[11]

---

11   Marc Ecko. *Unlabel: Selling You Without Selling Out.* Touchstone, 2013.

Wanda Alexis Alexander, founder and CEO of Horizon Consulting, Inc., has a similar perspective. She told me:

> 66 Sometimes when a vision is too specific, it is intimidating to your team and minimizes their ability to do their best, because they are always looking at a number and will compromise quality in order to hit that number. And if your team doesn't hit that specific number by the specific date you've set, then how does that impact them? You're going to have some defeated people, right?

Both good points. The size and scope of the quest matter far less than your commitment to achieve it. It doesn't matter how big or small of a difference you're making in the world; it matters more the difference you're making inside yourself.

CHAPTER 2

Inside Out, Not Outside In

"Your vision will become clear only when you look into your heart. Who looks outside, dreams. Who looks inside, awakens."

—*Carl Jung*

For your vision to be powerful, the results you want to achieve must be bigger than you. But since the quest starts with you, it must genuinely matter to you. It must tap into your passions and stubbornness, because if you're not committed to it, why should anyone else be?

Many of the world's most profitable companies and most innovative ideas came from regular people who saw something about the world that needed to change—something that should be better, something that irritated or frustrated them so much they felt inspired to take action.

Nick Swinmurn, the original founder of Zappos, started his online shoe company when he couldn't find a pair of Airwalks in the size and style he wanted at his local mall.[12] The Container Store also started with a small but powerful vision: to help people organize their lives. Frustrated with all the sugar in iced tea, Seth Goldman started making his own and sharing it with friends. People loved it, and there was nothing else like it on the market at the time, so he co-founded Honest Tea, which Coke now owns but he still runs.

On September 11, 2001, Jill Stelfox—then chief financial officer of Noblestar Systems—couldn't get in touch with staffers in

---

12 Meghan Cass. "Zappos Milestone: Q&A With Nick Swinmurn," Zappos Press Center. May 4, 2009. <http://about.zappos.com/press-center/media-coverage/zappos-milestone-qa-nick-swinmurn>.

the company's New York office. Then she received an email confirming a package she'd sent had been delivered. It occurred to her that something was wrong when she could easily locate a package, but not her staffers or even her children in case of emergency. Since then she has spearheaded several products aimed at keeping kids safe—including cell phone monitoring software for parents, as well as systems many D.C. schools now use to track students on busses and ensure faculty can quickly and easily make contact with parents in emergency situations.

Difficult life experience is another motivator for visionaries. After being crippled by tuberculosis as a teenager, Paul Bragg developed his own eating, breathing, and exercising program to rebuild his body into an ageless, tireless, pain-free citadel of health.[13] Then he opened the first health food store in America.

Maimah Karmo envisioned her nonprofit while battling breast cancer. During that time, her fiancé left her and their young daughter. Laid up in a hospital bed, fighting for her life, she couldn't pay her bills, feed her daughter, or handle her life. She was in her mid-30s—clueless about wellness and too young to have a nest egg. From her hospital bed, she started the Tigerlily Foundation to educate and support women under 40 who have breast cancer. One person, one mission, one hell of a success story.

Then there's Jas Boothe, founder of Final Salute. While serving in the U.S. military, she noticed an increasing number of homeless female veterans—many of whom were mothers who came back from war, wounded and/or traumatized, and simply couldn't get back on their feet. When Boothe did some research and learned that women vets were the fastest-growing segment of the homeless population, she decided to do something about it.[14] To date, Final Salute has opened three transitional homes for women vets and their children, and has provided housing and emergency financial assistance to more than 300 women vets across 15 states and territories.

---

13 "Paul Bragg, N.D., Ph.D. Lifestyle Extension Specialist, Health Crusader!" *Bragg.com*. <http://bragg.com/about/paul.html>.

14 Patricia Leigh Brown. "Trauma Sets Female Veterans Adrift Back Home," *The New York Times*. Feb. 27, 2013. <http://www.nytimes.com/2013/02/28/us/female-veterans-face-limbo-in-lives-on-the-street.html?pagewanted=all&_r=2&>.

All of these visionaries saw something that was missing or something that wasn't right, and decided to do something about it. Rallying others around the vision in their hearts was essential to being the change they wished to see in the world, so they found people who cared about what they cared about. And together, they changed things.

Get Stubborn

One of the best tests for the strength of your vision is how much you want it—how much passion it stirs inside of you and how adamant you are that it *must* be achieved. If your vision doesn't bring out the stubbornness in you, it certainly won't elicit a strong commitment from others. When you're clear about what taps into your stubbornness and invokes the "failure-is-not-an-option" mentality, you can push past perceived barriers and achieve what seems impossible.

Of course, stubbornness can also come back to bite you in the you-know-what. So let me be clear: Stubborn adherence to your vision is critical. But on the journey to achieving it, flexibility is also required.

Amazon founder Jeff Bezos knows how to strike the right balance. As Zach Bulygo writes:

> ❝ *According to Bezos, good entrepreneurs must be stubborn and flexible. When referring to Amazon, Bezos says, "We are stubborn on vision. We are flexible on details.*
>
> *Sticking to the vision is the first part, and being flexible about the tactics is the second part. Bezos adds, "If you're not stubborn, you'll give up on experiments too soon. And if you're not flexible, you'll pound your head against the wall and you won't see a different solution to a problem you're trying to solve."*[15]

Flexibility is also critical for enlisting others in your vision. People get in stubborn pursuit of visions they help to create. Give your employees the opportunity to be a part of the vision creation pro-

---

15 Zach Bulygo. "12 Business Lessons You Can Learn from Amazon Founder and CEO Jeff Bezos," *KISSmetrics.com*. Jan. 2013. <https://blog.kissmetrics.com/lessons-from-jeff-bezos/>.

cess, and watch as their personal accountability and sense of ownership naturally emerge.

Get Passionate

A vision is an outcome so clear and inspiring that the visionary will not stop until it is achieved. It is that incessant passion and focused action that inspires others to jump on board. Why? Because passion is contagious.

Effective leaders don't just know *what* they want to accomplish; they know *why* it's important and why they're working so hard to achieve it. When they share that passion, they attract others who want the same things and believe the same way they do.

The problem is, fewer than 20 percent of leaders have a strong sense of their own individual purpose.[16] And without knowing what drives you, it will be difficult to show the way for others.

Most people are waiting for someone to inspire them, rather than taking steps to inspire themselves. This reality is both a challenge and an opportunity for those who want to provoke greatness—both inside themselves and in others. People are hungry for inspiration, and if you can tap into that need, they'll line up to support your vision. But first, you must tap into what inspires *you*.

In other words, to provoke greatness, you must be willing to be provoked. The change and the challenge come from letting life touch you—letting your experiences, passion, and sense of purpose lead the way.

Without Inspiration, Visionaries Are Blind

Provokers simply cannot live lives void of inspiration and then expect to inspire others. Here are just a few ways to sprinkle inspiration into your day:

- **Join automobile university**—a phrase I first heard used by Zig Ziglar. Use your commute time to listen to inspirational CDs, podcasts, audiobooks, or TED Talks.

---

16 Nick Craig and Scott Snook. "From Purpose to Impact," *Harvard Business Review*. May 2014. <http://hbr.org/2014/05/from-purpose-to-impact/ar/1>.

- **Stop and smell the roses.** Spending time outside—gardening, hiking, bird watching, playing sports, or lying on a beach—is a great way to spur creativity and ground yourself emotionally.

- **Find your muse.** There is something magical that happens when I hear a musician belt out a beautiful song or watch a photographer who loves his craft get into the moment. The artist's passion elicits the same response in me, and I can't help but be inspired.

- **Take me out to the ballgame.** Watching athletes who are passionate about their sport—who love the game and train hard to be their very best—can also be an inspirational experience.

- **Get away from it all.** Travel is a great way to gain new perspectives and see things in a fresh light. Experiencing new cultures and seeing new parts of the world can open your mind to ideas you never considered.

- **Quiet the noise.** Meditation is a great way to slow your brain down and clear your head of all the thoughts that distract you and prevent inspiration.

For a longer list of ways to keep yourself inspired, visit www. MeasurableGreatness/HowToProvoke.

CHAPTER 3

Are You More Captivating than Angry Birds?

"When in doubt, make a fool of yourself. There is a microscopically thin line between being brilliantly creative and acting like the most gigantic idiot on earth. So what the hell, leap."

—Cynthia Heimel

Like attracts like. Just as passionate knitters, birdwatchers, video gamers, and chess players seem to find each other, so do people with other common passions and interests. When you know what inspires you and begin taking steps in the direction of your passion, others with common passions will emerge to help you get there.

Highly-motivated, innovative people with a passion for technology tend to seek opportunities with innovative, visionary companies such as Google, Facebook, or Apple. High-achievers who love food tend to be attracted to Whole Foods, Trader Joe's, and health food stores. Likewise, those who are passionate about the outdoors flock to companies like Recreational Equipment Inc. (REI), Patagonia, or Cabela's.

When you declare a strong and compelling vision like these companies have, you attract people who are similarly motivated to make a difference in your industry. On the other hand, when your vision is unclear, you attract people with the same lack of clarity, energy, and enthusiasm. So if your productivity, retention, and employee-engagement levels aren't where you want them to be, chances are that you haven't established and communicated a strong and compelling vision.

From Disengaged to Unstoppable

Consider the following example: My friend Stacey had been working with a new video game company for about six months when I asked her, "What's the vision for this game you're working on?"

"We don't really have a vision," Stacey said. "The CEO and another employee have been brainstorming about it for months, but they've yet to create an 'official' vision."

Then about a year into product development, the company hired a new creative director, Anthony. In just two weeks, Anthony created his own vision for the product, called an all-hands meeting to share his vision, and explained exactly how each department's contributions mattered.

"These guys usually sit in meetings, slumped over, playing Angry Birds on their phones," Stacey told me. "But ever since *that* meeting, they look like this..." She set her iPhone aside, pulled her chair up to the table, and started excitedly bouncing her legs. "When I asked a couple of the guys why they couldn't sit still, they said they were excited to get back to work."

That's the power of a vision!

From the Boardroom to the Summit

Companies lose countless dollars each year because of distracted, disengaged, unmotivated employees. Believe it or not, Angry Birds alone costs businesses up to $1.5 billion in lost wages.[17] But as addictive as game apps might be, when you have an inspiring vision, you can win their attention away from their smartphones and put it where it needs to be—on doing the work that supports the vision.

Why do more than 50,000 people risk their lives each year attempting to summit Mt. Kilimanjaro?[18] There are countless reasons people climb, but the most common response is related to their desire to achieve something great—something they'll always remember and that they can be remembered for.

The same is true for teams like Anthony's. I know several peo-

---

17 Jay Yarow. "Angry Birds Costing Businesses $1.5 Billion In Lost Wages," *Business Insider*. Sep. 14, 2011. <http://www.businessinsider.com/angry-birds-losses-2011-9>.

18 "Number of People Climbing Mount Kilimanjaro at Record High," *PRWeb.com*. Mar. 25, 2013. <http://www.prweb.com/releases/2013/3/prweb10559544.htm>.

ple in the video game industry. All of them talk about the same goal: to get "a successful title under my belt." They want to be able to tell people, "Hey, I worked on that," and to feel the sense of accomplishment that comes with creating something people enjoy.

By clearly defining his vision for the game (or "the summit") and tapping into the passions of his team members, Anthony didn't just capture their attention. He inspired them to work harder than ever to accomplish the vision. And it paid off.

Stacey later told me that before launching new products, video game companies often hire psychologists to ensure their products get the desired emotional response from customers. These doctors hook up electrodes to beta testers, and track when and how they respond while playing—when a certain level is too frustrating or not challenging enough.

When the results came back for this particular game, it was clear Anthony knew what he was doing. "We started getting a huge increase in the emotional responses we were looking for once there was a vision for the game," Stacey told me. "You can actually see the difference in the results before Anthony was hired and after he came on board."

So have you identified *your summit*? Does your team know exactly where you're taking them and why it's so important to get there? And just as importantly, do they understand the roles they have to play along the way?

What's Your Summit?

It doesn't matter if you're the CEO, a first-tier manager, or a brand new employee with a clear and compelling vision; you have the power to captivate and create extraordinary results. Consider the following when defining your summit:

- **Do your homework.** Before Anthony could create something exciting to aim for, he had to understand what each team was doing and why. He had to understand the product they were working on, the audience they were creating it for, and what excited him about the product.

- **Go big.** An exciting vision must be something that will not only make money, but also capture and retain the team's attention and devotion.
- **Acknowledge.** People don't trust change, unless they understand why it's happening. To get his team on board, Anthony had to acknowledge where they'd been and help them visualize where they could go.
- **Electrify.** The most clearly articulated vision means nothing if it doesn't truly excite its creator. If Anthony hadn't cared about these people and the product, his team would have sensed that, and it's unlikely they would have been excited. But leaders who are genuinely passionate about what they've set out to achieve have a contagious positive energy.
- **Reinforce.** One inspiring meeting would not have kept the attention of employees long-term. According to Stacey, Anthony continually communicates and reinforces his vision, both with new and existing employees.

For a step-by-step guide to vision setting, visit www.MeasurableGreatness.com/HowToProvoke.

CHAPTER 4

Can They Hear Your Music?

"The great leaders I've studied are all people whose energy and drive are directed outward. It's not about themselves. It's about something greater than themselves."

—Jim Collins

Have you ever watched an exceptionally talented orchestra perform? Each person plays a different instrument and different notes, but they're not just guessing at what they're supposed to play or when they're supposed to play it. They take their cues from the conductor, who brings all the different sounds together into one beautiful, consistent piece of music. If even one musician doesn't understand how his or her part fits in with the rest, the song will be missing an important layer or the rhythm will be all wrong, and suddenly the beautiful music will just be noise.

Likewise, when you lead a team, everyone plays a different role and does a different job, but when you add all those efforts together, you get progress toward the vision. Provokers go beyond setting and communicating an inspiring vision. They ensure team members understand their individual roles—how their individual VOICEs add to the song they're playing.

How do you do that? It all depends on the person. Some people naturally see the big picture and understand how it all fits together. But most people need more guidance. They need help connecting the dots and understanding what they're supposed to do and why.

Three Types of Dancers
Think about a time when you've attended a wedding or other event where there was dancing. You might have noticed three types

of dancers. I call them Freestylers, Groovers, and Swatchers.

Freestylers jump on the dance floor the minute music starts and bust a move. Some are fun to watch; others are just plain funny.

Groovers are a little shyer. With some encouragement, they'll get out there and groove with the music. But they stay in their little circles, careful not to dance with too much enthusiasm, lest they embarrass themselves.

Then there are Swatchers. These talented dancers sit and watch, or swatch the dance floor, patiently waiting for that song to come on so they can jump in and jam it out. By that song, I mean some sort of line-dancing song—the one everybody seems to have carefully studied on YouTube and spent hours perfecting in the safety of their homes (think Gangnam Style, Cupid Shuffle, or the Electric Slide). These songs, with their structured movements, give relatively shy dancers the courage to shake their booties.

The minute one of these jams come on, Swatchers shoot to the dance floor. Groovers suddenly gain some rockin' movement in their hips that wasn't there before. And the Freestylers either leave the dance floor or find a way to move with the rhythm of the Groovers and Swatchers.

When the song ends, the Swatchers quickly make their way back to their seats; the Groovers hang out for the beginning of the next song; and the Freestylers return to the dance floor with reckless abandon.

Most of us want to dance, to let the music move through us and really get into the song. Yet most of us won't do it in public, at least not without structure or someone to assure us that we're "doing it right."

Show Them the Right Moves

Most leaders want their teams to dance—to achieve great things together—but they don't clearly articulate what success looks like. Very few dancers are natural Freestylers. The vast majority are Swatchers. They want to succeed and are capable of success, but they don't understand the rules. They don't understand exactly what they need to do in order to successfully contribute to the vision.

Don't misunderstand me. I am not suggesting you microman-age your team. Instead, help them understand what they're aiming to achieve, why their contributions are important to the company's vision and mission, and how to consistently improve their skills.

Every company dances to the beat of its own unique song. Help your team learn how to groove with you, and soon they'll be tapping their feet faster, holding their chests higher, and adding their VOICEs to yours.

CHAPTER 5

Calling a Ceasefire: How Vision Unites Your Team

"Diversity: the art of thinking independently together."
—Malcolm Forbes

How do you know if your team is engaged in your vision? One clear indicator is whether they're working together to accomplish it, or too busy bickering to collaborate.

On average, supervisors and managers spend 30 to 40 percent of their time dealing with conflicts in the workplace. While it seems absurd that grownup professionals can't get along, it is human nature to allow our differences to separate us, unless something else brings us together.

Just consider the havoc that generational differences alone can wreak on a workplace. Gen Y has been part of the workforce for more than a decade. By 2020, it will constitute half of all workers; yet the generational conflict is still going strong in many organizations. Why? Contrary to popular belief, conflict does not stem from our differences. It's a result of our insecurities.

Purpose and vision unite people in spite of their differences. Simply put, if you don't give people something to rally around, they will stand apart—and seek to stand out by hoarding and hiding information.

The Source of the Conflict

According to researchers from the University of North Carolina, generational stereotypes are scientifically unfounded. While we may have different communication styles, interests, and methods, we think about work in the same terms. We share the same motivators, commitment levels, and desire for opportunities. We also have the same perceptions of leadership, organizational climate, and work attitudes. "Stereotypes limit contributions of people of all ages and organizational levels," the report concludes, "and can hurt collaboration, production, workplace relationships, and individual self-perception."

You won't get any arguments from Chris, a young Australian man who shared the following story with me:

I recently participated in a do-it-yourself workshop at a major hardware chain, and a young staff member came in and turned on the TV. When the host asked why, he said the boss told him to do so. "But we don't need it," said the host. The younger guy shrugged and left. He truly seemed at a loss as to why he was doing it; he wasn't being cheeky.

The only other participant in the workshop—a Boomer, like our host—asked, "Who's he?"

The host replied, "He's a smartass."

"Oh yeah," said the other participant, "one of these whizz-bang kids who thinks he can change the world in five minutes." The host agreed. I didn't say anything but I felt disgusted.

Chris then put his finger on exactly what was going on here: "I think [generational conflict] stems from the insecurity some seasoned professionals feel...that somehow their positions or status will become redundant or diminished because of the 'whizz-bang kids.'"

I agree with Chris. When seasoned professionals are worried they haven't done enough with their careers or will soon be outdated, they are likely to resent younger workers. They might come across as cocky know-it-alls, but they're really just afraid they're not good enough.

On the flip side, young pros have their own insecurities to contend with—uncertainty about the future, a lack of mentors and training, and having to hear seasoned pros say how much harder it was for them and how Millennials' expectations are too high. No wonder the generations are still butting heads!

Something in Common

The different generations aren't the only ones who can't play nice at work. There are many types of diversity in the workplace—gender, race, religion, political affiliation, sexual orientation, cultural heritage, life experiences, personality traits, and even work styles. Each of these differences can stir up futile battles and unproductive sabotage, unless teams have fearless leaders who give them a reason to reach.

What if the two hardware-store employees in Chris's story saw themselves as valuable contributors to the long-term success of the organization? How might that interaction have played out differently if the Boomer host had seen the young professional as a valuable asset to the organization's success—his comrade in an important quest?

As John Mackey and Raj Sisodia write in Conscious Capitalism, "When all stakeholders are aligned around a common higher purpose, they are less likely to care only about their immediate, narrowly defined self-interest."

With a common vision to rally around, people stop criticizing each other because of their differences and start looking for ways to capitalize on the unique assets each person brings to the table.

HIGHLIGHTS
SECTION 1: VISION

1. A compelling vision is clear, specific, measurable, and often has a date associated with it.

2. A powerful vision inspires the people working to achieve it and makes them feel like they're part of something that matters.

3. One of the best tests for the strength of your vision is how much you want it—how much passion it stirs inside of you and how adamant you are that it be achieved. That incessant passion and focused action inspire others to jump on board.

4. It's not enough to simply set an inspiring vision and communicate it to your team. You also have to help them understand their individual roles in achieving the vision and why their contributions are important.

5. If you don't give your team a compelling vision to rally around, they will stand apart—and seek to stand out by hoarding and hiding information.

Section 2: Ownership

Ownership: Accepting full responsibility for results

If vision is about seeing, ownership is about accepting full responsibility for what you see.

One of the best litmus tests for your VOICE is the results you're getting from your team. When you compare your desired results to your actual outcomes, you'll clearly see your opportunities to grow. Alas, it's a never-ending process. The bigger you dream, the more challenges you'll set out to accomplish, and the more opportunities you will have to learn about your own talents and shortcomings.

I recently hosted a dinner with eight highly-acclaimed CEOs from the Washington D.C. area to discuss my favorite topic: provoking greatness. To start things off, we went around the table so participants could introduce themselves and share what they were hoping to get out of the discussion.

When it was Eduardo's turn, he explained, "My greatest challenge is getting my leadership team to listen to each other. They talk over each other and refuse to hear what the others are saying."

Several minutes later, as another CEO was sharing his vision and explaining what's at stake if he doesn't accomplish it, Eduardo interrupted him and shifted the conversation back to his team's poor listening skills. The irony was lost on Eduardo, but not on the rest of us. His team was clearly following their CEO's lead!

The next time you find yourself complaining about certain behaviors in your employees, stop and consider whether you might be unconsciously reinforcing those bad habits. Rather than wonder why they're behaving a particular way, ask yourself, "What changes do I need to make so that I see new behaviors in the people around me?"

Are you to blame for the shortcomings of everyone on your team or for every bad behavior they exhibit? Of course not. But owning full responsibility for their results is the only place of real power. When you take ownership for bringing about the outcomes you want, you have the power to influence real change and growth. When you place ownership on them, you're left at the mercy of some outside force or their whims, and you give away your power to provoke.

Provoking greatness requires:

- Owning your beliefs
- Owning your own greatness
- Owning your part in bringing forth their greatness
- Owning your results—and theirs
- Empowering your team to take ownership of their greatness and their results

In this section, we'll discuss the life-altering, results-enhancing benefits of owning every success and failure you and your team have ever had, or will ever have.

CHAPTER 6

Change Your Mindset, Change Your Outcomes

"This is how humans are: We question all our beliefs, except for the ones we really believe, and those we never think to question."
—Orson Scott Card

If you're not getting the desired results from your team, consider whether your perspective needs shifting. If you believe they'll underperform, that's what you'll see. But if you believe they will succeed, you'll have the power to help them do it.

Perspective is powerful. Consider this: When Michelle Obama wears a rockin' new dress, one person might say, "Wow, that's a sexy dress," another might say, "She looks like a school teacher in that dress," and yet another might say, "She looks professional." She's the same woman, wearing the same dress. Yet each person's opinion stems directly from his or her perspective. Of course, none of their opinions are "right," except to them.

Likewise, one leader might look at an employee and say, "He is lazy, incompetent, and useless," while another leader might look at the same person and say, "He is talented, ready for more challenges, and excellent with customer service."

Why does one person see "sexy" while another sees "professional?" Why does one leader see problems while another sees potential? Because we all see through the lens of our own unique experiences, challenges, and successes.

Take Control of Your Perceptions

Understanding this puts you in a position of greater power. When you agree that you're seeing based on your perspective, you have the power to broaden it. When you think what you're seeing or experiencing is outside of you, you remain a prisoner in your own mind, unable to change or affect your outcomes.

A few months ago, my friend Joel went to the doctor for a physical. On his way to the appointment, he got a phone call with some stressful news. Thirty minutes later when a nurse took his blood pressure, it was 195/120.

The doctor was concerned and wanted to put Joel on medication immediately. "No, no," Joel said. "Give me a few minutes. I just got some bad news."

About 15 minutes later, when the nurse ran the test again, his blood pressure had come down, but not enough. "We're going to have to do something about this," the doctor said.

"No, it's just stress-related," Joel again insisted. "I need 15 more minutes."

The doctor agreed to give him one last chance. This time Joel sat there purposefully focusing his attention on thoughts of his children. He imagined playing with them, relaxing, and enjoying time with his family. Fifteen minutes later his blood pressure had dropped to 135/85 (well within the normal range), and they sent him home without medication.

This is the power of our minds. Our thoughts shape our realities, and that's great news. Because as Joel proved, we have the ability to create, shift, or ignore them.

What Were You Expecting?

The Secret, Think and Grow Rich, and The Science of Getting Rich—each of these international bestsellers has this message in common: What you think about, you bring about.

Neuroscientists have even given this phenomenon a name. The "Expectancy Theory" states that the brain patterns created by our expectations can be just as real as those created by real-world events. For example, in one study, a group of hotel maids were told their work was a good cardio workout and burned calories. After several weeks, these maids had lost weight and lowered their cholesterol more than maids who didn't expect their work to be good exercise.

Understanding this concept is critical for leaders. If you're expecting your team to be lazy, unwilling to pay their dues, incompetent, or lacking enthusiasm, you'll find plenty of examples to confirm those beliefs. But if you focus on their talents, you'll discover those as well.

I'm not suggesting you ignore challenges or turn a blind eye when employees mess up. In fact, challenges and mistakes can be great opportunities to learn, develop employees, and strengthen your team. Doing so requires feedback (which we'll discuss in detail in the next section).

That said, there's a difference between dealing with an unpleasant situation and expecting things to go badly. To paraphrase the old saying, we should plan for the worst, but expect the best—in ourselves, in situations, and in other people—because we'll find exactly what we're looking for.

Case in point: At a Foundation dinner for the National Speakers Association, I met Dave, a fellow speaker and reporter. When I asked what he does for a living, he said, "I expose the terrible things companies do in and around Dallas."

After sharing a few specific examples of telephone, gas, and electric companies that have treated customers poorly, he added, "I get upwards of 30 emails a day with stories from people who have had terrible experiences."

When he asked about my line of work, I said proudly, "I'm a provoker of greatness. I work with leaders to show them how to create environments where people of all different generations want to excel, collaborate, and innovate."

"All leadership coaches are terrible!" he said. "Just awful."

His honesty was both humorous and fascinating. "You think I'm terrible?" I asked, with a giant smile to let him know I wasn't offended.

"Well...I mean...just look around at how many terrible leaders there are," he stammered. "Clearly you leadership coaches aren't doing your job!"

I couldn't help but laugh. Of course Dave would think that way. He's trained to look for what's not working and then report on it. Why would he notice the leaders who are leading well or the coaches who help them? He's not looking for them.

The reason Dave only notices terrible leaders is the same reason many leaders fail to tap into the greatness of the people on their teams. Or worse yet, they lose talented team members, who either find employment elsewhere or start their own companies.

Most companies are in a constant battle to attract the best of the best, because the leadership team is unwilling to see the talent they already have and to make it their business to provoke it. No leader wants to fail to get results. Likewise, people want to do their best work. They might just need a little direction and someone willing to see past their problems and focus on their potential.

Change Your Expectations, Change Your Results

Ever heard the story about the teacher who thought her students' locker numbers were their I.Q. scores?

At the beginning of the year, she was assigned a class full of out-of-control little heathens who seemed unteachable. She started to worry that some or most of them might have learning disorders or mental deficiencies. Feeling bad for them (and for herself), she snuck into the principal's office and did something she wasn't supposed to do—looked at her students' I.Q. numbers. Surprisingly enough, the majority of her students were extremely bright, even brilliant.

Believing her students were capable of so much more than what she'd been seeing, she began to treat them that way and to insist on getting more from them. They rose to the occasion and eventually became the best-behaved, highest-performing class in their grade level.

When the principal asked the teacher her secret, she confessed that she'd snuck a peak at their I.Q. scores. The principal surprised her by explaining that the numbers she'd seen were actually her students' locker numbers. But the distinction no longer mattered. She had already believed in them and treated them as though they were capable of greatness...and so they were.

If you're expecting your team to be top performers, and if you trust them enough to give them opportunities to learn, they'll rise to the occasion. If you expect them to goof off and treat them as though they can't be trusted, you'll have a self-fulfilling leadership catastrophe on your hands.

So if you cannot see their potential, and you cannot shift your perspective about them, help them find other opportunities. Your perspective is your reality. Choose to see their talents, or let someone else, with another lens, see it and pull it out.

CHAPTER 7

Failing to Fail

"Many of life's failures are people who did not realize how close they were to success when they gave up."

—Thomas Edison

Believing in yourself and your vision is just as important as believing in your team, if not more so. To be the kind of person others want to follow, you must think you are worth believing in and following.

Self-doubt is a leader's worst enemy. Insecurity is part of being human, but if we don't believe in ourselves, how can we ever expect to inspire others? Just as importantly, when we doubt ourselves, we live in fear and don't take the risks that could get us to that next level.

Fight Your Fear with Fanaticism
As much as we like to think that talented visionaries simply have it all together, they don't. They're subject to the same fears of messing up as the rest of us. What sets them apart is the ability to keep going, despite any doubts or unpleasant feelings.

When Fairbank first started Capital One, he wasn't sure his ideas would work. After months without being able to deliver a return for his investors, he realized that each day could be his last, for himself and his dream of Capital One. Rather than give up and say, "I guess I can't do it after all," he stayed focused—and fanatical—about his vision. And he surrounded himself with other leaders who were just as passionate.

"The folks sitting around the same table as me are fanatical," he says. "They see the result they want to create and will do what it takes to make it happen. Obstacles must give way."

With that kind of "failure is not an option" attitude, it's no wonder Fairbanks's company became a multibillion-dollar organization. Of course, even when you're fanatical, negativity creeps in, either through your self-talk or from outsiders. But the quickest, most effective way to show pessimism the door is to remember what you're aiming to achieve and why it's important. Without the belief that you can achieve remarkable outcomes, or a strong and compelling reason to succeed, pessimism will take you down. Watch the thoughts you're choosing to focus on; they show up in your results.

Embrace Failure

Failure is a mindset, which is why successful people consider failure a good thing. When you expect to fail—knowing you will get back up again—failure stops being scary and actually strengthens your ability to dream bigger. Rather than being the end of your dreams, it becomes simply a new and better starting point—one where you're more informed about what not to do, and therefore one step closer to figuring out what to do.

When Thomas Edison had been trying for quite some time to invent the light bulb, a young reporter boldly asked if he felt like a failure. Edison famously told him, "I have not failed. I have just found 10,000 ways that won't work." Not long after, Edison had a working light bulb in his hands.

Fairbank says embracing failure also sets a good example for your team and helps create a culture of innovation. He explains:

> ❝ If you want an organization of people that are willing to stick their necks out and take a risk and really go for it, you can't have an environment where there are public hangings over a single mistake. Part of living up to one's potential is getting out of your own way and having the courage to really go for it. People want to do that, and they are attracted to leaders who let them—who aren't afraid to fail and who don't mind if they do too.

Helping people reach their greatness requires taking steps into unchartered territories, tinkering, failing, and ultimately finding out what doesn't work in order to discover what does. Those who stay too comfortable don't take risks, so they fail to change or grow, leaving themselves wide open to irrelevancy. This is as true in the science of innovation as it is in the science of provocation.

Blockbuster failed to fail, choosing to rest on its laurels and not take the risks necessary for innovation. Meanwhile Netflix—with its mail-order DVD rentals and instant videos—knew the future of movie viewing was changing. Netflix had a cheaper business model with much less overhead than traditional movie rental stores, and it catered to its increasingly tech-savvy, impatient consumers. By the time Blockbuster started offering the same options, the damage had already been done. The industry had changed, and Blockbuster went the way of 8-Track and Beta players. Throughout the early 2000s, when Netflix had great ideas but no profits to boast of yet, Blockbuster had multiple chances to purchase Netflix for $50 million, but passed. Today Netflix is a multibillion-dollar corporation with more than 50 million members around the world.

Companies and leaders who aren't afraid to take risks know that many of their ideas won't pan out and that not every product or solution will be embraced by customers—in essence, that they will fail. But the ones who truly believe in the value they have to offer, and who know that failure is a necessary steppingstone on the path to success, are the ones who continue to grow, drive innovation, and inspire people. They attract people who are passionate about the vision, and who want to take personal ownership for helping to make the vision a reality.

CHAPTER 8

Take Ownership for Leadership

"We awaken in others the same attitude of mind we hold toward them."
—Elbert Hubbard

To provoke greatness in your team, you must believe it is your job to do so—that developing people is your most important role. Yet far too many leaders either don't know how to lead or would rather not be bothered.

Take Paul, for example. An executive in the education field, he actually told me, "My title is too big for this piddly crap. It's beneath me."

Paul was frustrated with Tina, a woman he'd promoted three weeks prior to our meeting. "She's incompetent," he said. "I'm removing her from the position."

"It's only been three weeks," I pointed out. "Maybe she needs a little guidance and coaching."

Over the next five minutes, Paul listed countless reasons Tina did not deserve his attention. "These are not the kinds of issues someone at my level should be dealing with," he said. "I'm moving her under someone who has time to manage her."

When I asked Paul about his responsibility as the leader of a talented group of people, he responded, "At this level in the game, I should be dealing with much higher-level responsibilities, like building a name for our organization."

I wonder what would happen to the name of Paul's organization—and his own reputation—if he understood that his team is the gateway to creating a powerful brand. Brands aren't something you build. Meaningful, long-lasting brands are something you become, with the help of a dedicated, loyal team that cares about the success of your company. But they won't care a flip about you or your vision if you don't care about them.

If you want to pull out the best in your team, resist the temptation to lead from ego or fear. To provoke greatness, you must lead from love.

Forget Fear...

Employees have a hard time caring about an organization's success when they're too busy worrying about their own livelihoods. I recently experienced the result of fearful leadership firsthand. While walking up a steep hill next to my old apartment building, I ran into a solid, orange beam—head first. I was moving at full speed, messing with my phone (naturally!), and hit the beam with such force that my phone went flying into the bushes. I dropped to the ground, and my water bottle rolled down the hill.

Disoriented, I tried to figure out what the heck had flown out of nowhere and smacked me in the head. Lying there on the sidewalk, with tears rushing down my cheeks, I saw the orange beam of the construction lift and instantly got angry. Why weren't there any cones or signs to warn me? I thought, applying pressure to my throbbing head.

I lay there for two solid minutes before anyone came to check on me. Finally one of the workers approached. "You OK?" he asked.

"No, my head hurts," I said and then angrily asked about the lack of warning. Granted, looking up when walking helps to avoid such collisions, but cones would have helped.

"I was just around the corner," he pleaded.

"That didn't help me. You're supposed to have cones out."

He shrugged his shoulders and avoided making eye contact, clearly fearful he might be in trouble. "I was just around the corner," he repeated. "I was coming right back."

Rather than continue this circular dialogue, I pulled myself up off the ground and headed to the apartment building's main office, where I asked for the phone number of the man who owns the construction company.

The owner apologized profusely and agreed his crew should

have put cones out, so I asked him to do me two favors. "Please be sure they understand the importance of putting cones out when the lift is that low," I said. "Also, please encourage them to be sympathetic and apologetic, and to own full responsibility for mistakes."

"In our weekly meetings, we go over exactly what to say in these situations," he assured me. "But they continue to react that way. They're afraid I'll make them pay. I never do, but to ensure they're careful, I let them think I will."

Now I completely understood the problem. You can't keep people fearful and then expect them to react with kindness. Your team will respond in accordance with what you're provoking in them. When you use fear as a motivator, you fail to provoke greatness. Instead you provoke fear, anxiety, and stress—all of which are toxic for your workplace culture, your customer relations, and your bottom line.

The cost of stress alone is astounding. Work-related stress costs U.S. companies more than $300 billion annually as a result of accidents, absenteeism, employee turnover, diminished productivity, and health care costs. And stressed out, disengaged employees are not who you want talking to customers. If you want your team to show kindness, you have to show them kindness. If you want them to treat customers with sympathy and respect, you have to do the same with them.

Mistakes happen in all areas of business, but when your employees are afraid of your reaction if they mess up, you not only discourage growth and innovation. You also negatively impact your customers' experiences.

...Lead from Love

On the other hand, when employees know you truly care about them, they'll walk through fire for you. But here's the thing: You can't lead from both fear and love, because as Elizabeth Kübler-Ross so famously pointed out, "If we're in fear, we are not in a place of love. When we're in a place of love, we cannot be in a place of fear." Fear is, at its core, the absence of love. So as a leader, you must make a choice.

Jack, the CEO of a rather large corporation in Baltimore, knew several of his team members were capable of producing at much higher levels than they had been. But he was struggling to help them improve their performance.

Knowing Jack had set a clear, inspiring vision—the first step to keeping employees engaged and productive—I asked him to share more about his specific challenge.

"As CEO, I have retention and revenue numbers I must reach to continue achieving new levels of success," he said. "There are a few key people on my team who don't seem to care enough about succeeding in these goals."

"Do you care about their success?" I asked.

His answer sent chills up my spine. "No," he said.

His willingness to be authentic, even when the truth might seem like the "wrong" answer, was nice. I thanked him for his honesty and told him that his solution was simple: "If you want them to care about their work, you have to care about their success."

He fired back, "I have real goals I must meet! They need to understand that if they don't do their jobs, they might lose them."

"So you're using fear as a driver?" I asked.

"Yes, and I've seen it work in the military for years."

"While fear might be an appropriate, effective motivator in some situations, it's not working for you right now, is it?" I asked.

Silence echoed through the long stretch of empty chairs that lined the narrow section of the restaurant where we had already finished our meal. Having seen how respectfully Jack interacted with several individuals on his team, and knowing that caring about others is innate for most people, I knew Jack had it in him to be a more compassionate leader.

"Caring for others is part of who you are," I told him. "Consider releasing your fear, staying clear on your vision, and showing your team that you care about their success."

You Reap What You Sow

As John C. Maxwell so beautifully puts it, "People don't care how much you know until they know how much you care." If you want your team to care—about their work, about the vision, or about the company's success—you have to care about them. Plain and simple, you reap what you sow.

Most leaders expect people to care just because they pay them to do so. Some even spend hundreds of thousands of dollars each year to have someone else bring them caring employees. Then they scratch their heads in disbelief when those employees leave. Rather than address the lack of caring inside of themselves and their companies, they pay consultants to come in, evaluate the culture, identify the issues, and fix them. Then they pay thousands of dollars again to have more caring people brought into the company. "I want results," they say. "I want people who care about their jobs enough to drive results!"

Of course, we know what happens next. Those caring people care enough about themselves to find employers who actually care about them.

This is how far too many companies operate. More than 70 percent of employees don't feel appreciated or valued by their employers. Seventy percent! This reality brings with it a huge opportunity for leaders who get it right.

I'll never forget Frank, a highly successful sales executive I met years ago at Hartsfield–Jackson International Airport. After learning a bit about the medical devices he sells, I asked if he loved his job.

"No," Frank said. He explained that his company had spent thousands of dollars to recruit him just a couple years back—including several interviews, dinners, flights, etc. But now he was looking for another job. "They did everything to get me and nothing to keep me."

"What would they need to do to keep you?" I asked.

"Help me see where I have room for improvement, give me opportunities to expand my skill set and network, and offer me opportunities to have a seat at the executive table. I want to learn, but I'm having trouble figuring out how to both do my job well and improve."

In other words, Frank wanted his employer to care about him

and his success. As with all relationships, caring comes in the form of listening, sharing time, asking questions, providing guidance, taking feedback, making introductions, sharing resources, sharing battle wounds, and looking out for the best interests of the people around you. When you do those things, you'll have a pile of qualified applicants who care about your mission, and who will own full responsibility for their part in making it a success.

Get Curious: 5 Questions Provokers of Greatness Can Answer

In order to help employees grow and succeed, great leaders get curious about what makes them tick, what gets them excited, and what they truly want out of their careers. Here are five questions great provokers can answer about their team members:

1. **What skills would they like to gain in the next six months to a year?**

   While many people don't know where they want to go with their careers, most have an idea of what skills they'd like to gain. This information will give you the fuel to ignite their hidden passions.

2. **What experiences would they like to gain in the next six months to a year?**

   You'd be amazed at what happens to some people's commitment and motivation levels when given an opportunity to sit in on high-profile meetings, shadow leaders they admire, or just try something outside of their job descriptions.

3. **What do they need to be more effective in their jobs?**

   Unless asked, many people refrain from sharing

their challenges, or they share in ways that are toxic to workplace morale. Taking the time each week to ask allows you to address potential problems before they become bigger issues.

4. Do they feel like part of a community when they come to work?

Most people work harder with people they know, respect, value, and maybe even enjoy being around. Ensure your employees feel connected to each other and the vision.

5. Do they love their jobs?

Most people think work has to feel like...well, work. Yet the most productive employees have fun at the office. They love what they do and are happy about how they contribute.

For more on learning what matters to your team, visit www. MeasurableGreatness.com / HowToProvoke.

CHAPTER 9

Empower Them to Provoke Their Own Greatness

"Leadership is communicating to people their worth and potential so clearly that they come to see it in themselves."

—Stephen Covey, from *The 9th Habit*

Once you see your team's potential, believe in them, care about their success, and know what makes them tick, you're well on your way to provoking greatness. But the end goal is to empower them to do it for themselves.

Sure, some people see their own talent, but others don't. So while most leaders go searching for A+ performers, remarkable provokers uncover them. They can't help but see untapped potential and enjoy provoking it.

Help Them See What You See

Cars don't slide into ditches or crash into each other because of a few flakes of snow. But once snow and ice have accumulated, the conditions can quite literally cause a 15-car pileup.

Words of encouragement work the same way. Some people have heard words of affirmation thousands of times throughout their lives: "There's nothing you cannot do. You're talented. Do more of that; you light up when you're doing it. You are wonderful to be around, and I appreciate you." In fact, they've heard such things so often that they buy into the idea. Their self-talk mimics the words above, and because they believe such positive things about themselves and their potential, those things become true.

The problem is that many of us rarely, if ever, hear those words. Somehow we make it into our careers hearing quite the opposite, and we believe it. Of course, most people want to live to their potential. And nearly all of us are already A+ performers. The vast majority simply don't know it…yet!

We haven't had the benefit of others pointing out our gifts. That's why, according to Zig Ziglar's research, most people's self-talk is about 77 percent negative. We don't see our talents as assets, nor do we know how to use them to build something really great that leaves us beaming with pride.

This is where provokers of greatness come in. These people (sometimes leaders and often extraordinary friends and mentors) see beneath the haze of lies we've bought into, point out our talents, provide a vision of what's possible, and stand in support of us until we also see this truth.

Just like a few flakes of snow, delivered after weeks of warm weather, will melt away before accumulating, we simply don't slide into excellence without a barrage of positive words, actions, and successes.

The great news is that they do add up over time—and begin to stick.

Insist on Their Greatness

Telling your people about the greatness you see in them can be a powerful motivator, but it's just as important to prove you mean it by insisting they live up to that potential.

Not long ago, my parents came to visit. While we were driving back to my place from the Lexington Market in Baltimore, Maryland, my car's "tire pressure low" light came on again. I had refilled that tire three times in the past week, so how could it possibly be low again?

I had begrudgingly decided I would need a new tire when my dad, a mechanic for 50 years, said, "Why don't you get the tire checked, Misti? Maybe it just has a leak and needs to be repaired."

I hadn't even thought of that! So I went to the Merchant Tire Store in Towson, Maryland, where they found a leak that simply needed to be plugged. My tire wasn't ready to be retired after all.

Thankfully, my neglected tire didn't leave me stranded by the roadside, which was lucky, because it had zero pressure left when I got to the tire store. As it turns out, the right amount of pressure is what makes tires perform at their best. Go figure!

The same is true of teams; they need the right amount of pressure and inspiration to perform at their best. One of the definitions of inspiration is "to breathe life into," which is exactly what most people need to perform at higher levels. They need more air, and less demanding and firing. And they want someone to provoke them into revealing their greatness.

When employees aren't meeting expectations, leaders often replace, rather than reignite. Instead of looking into what might be causing the lackluster performance, they think, "These people are just not committed enough. They're complacent...or unwilling to pay their dues."

Maybe they simply need a tune-up—i.e., someone to care enough about their success and contributions to ask about their goals, whether they're enjoying the work, and what experiences/skills they'd like to gain. Leaders who investigate the source of the problem, rather than slap a new tire on the car, end up with the most committed, engaged, and fired-up employees.

Yes, I got lazy about my tire without even realizing I was doing so. Because my car was relatively new, I assumed it should be performing better. I didn't want to take the time to go the tire store. I just wanted the thing to fix itself. So I kept wasting energy refilling a tire that was in dire need of attention.

Once my tire got the love it needed, the light stayed off, and it performed perfectly. When you give your team the attention they need, the warning signs—complacency, lack of performance, complaining—will disappear, allowing for just the right pressure to provoke their greatness.

Actions Speak Louder Than Words

Commit to performing a simple empowering action just three times each day for someone on your team. By the end of the month, you`ll have created a cascade of ownership, teamwork, accountability, and innovation. The following are some specific ideas to get you started:

- **Delegate.** This gives team members opportunities to perform new tasks, while allowing you to focus on your most important job—leadership.

- **Stop attending important meetings alone.** Board meetings, client meetings, and special events can be great learning opportunities for your high-potential employees.

- **Help them reach their career ambitions.** Look for ways to help your team members reach their career goals and move your organization forward.

- **Tell them how their contributions matter.** Talk to individuals about their role in your company's mission and how their contributions impact the bottom line.

- **Speak up when your team has room to grow.** Having candid, productive conversations about performance is critical to powerful leadership.

- **Reward successes.** Don't get too busy to celebrate and reward individual and team successes.

- **Help them keep learning.** Research and share an interesting, short article that's relevant to the work your team is doing. Record a video that teaches employees how to do something useful. Provide new training, or suggest career-development books worth reading.

- **Volunteer together.** Rally your team to help a non-profit in a significant way.

- **Make connections.** Introduce an outstanding employee to someone influential—another employee, department head, client, or leader.

- **Relate to them.** Share a story with your team about a mistake you made, and tell how you used what you learned from that experience to bounce back.

For more ways to empower your team, visit www.MeasurableGreatness.com/HowToProvoke.

CHAPTER 10

Don't Hog the Ownership

"Before you are a leader, success is all about growing yourself. When you become a leader, success is all about growing others."

—Jack Welch

To provoke greatness, you must see yourself as the one responsible for your team's results. Any shift in ownership away from yourself causes you to lose power and the ability to effect change. Likewise, it's critical that your team also take full responsibility for the outcomes they create. This doesn't just lighten your load. It creates a team of self-motivated people with a stake in the game. This is the holy grail of talent management.

Listening to, and acting on, their ideas is a key way to increase ownership on your team. Rather than opt for the all-too-common "my way or the highway" approach, consider the impact of "people support that which they help to create." People are more dedicated to solving problems when they help to define the solutions. They push harder to accomplish goals they help to set.

Hear Them Out

I saw this lesson unfold last year at an annual event The Washington Business Journal hosts, honoring 25 of the region's most influential women (a.k.a., Women Who Mean Business).

As a past honoree, I have the privilege of being invited each year. These gatherings always begin with wine and appetizers while attendees mix and mingle. At some point, Alex Orfinger, publisher of the Journal, attempts to wrangle the roomful of women and introduce our sponsor, Capital One. A representative from Capital One then welcomes us, introduces the new honorees, and provides a few conversation starters (as if powerful business women need that!). Nonetheless, the topics are always interesting, and I enjoy hearing the diverse perspectives these questions provoke.

The 2013 question: "What can our group do to help deal with the challenges local businesses are facing as a result of the government shutdown?"

At first the answer was pretty much what you'd expect: Call your Congressman incessantly and pray. Then one lady stood up and agreed to give $500 to the Emergency Assistance Fund, a non-profit that helps those in need during times like these.

As soon as she sat down, a woman from a local energy company stood up and talked about how much her company is doing from a volunteer perspective, and then added, "And I'll personally give $1,000."

I was shocked! While I have no clue about her personal finances, $1,000 is no small lump of cash to be handing out on a whim. The government shutdown certainly wasn't our responsibility, nor was helping struggling companies. Yet after the initial offer, hands started flying up.

Clearly unprepared, one of the ladies from Capital One grabbed a pen and napkin to write down the names and amounts promised. She couldn't quite keep up, so support staff from the Journal jumped in to help. Together we raised more than $16,000 in less than 10 minutes.

As I reflect on this story, I wonder what would have happened if the hosts had suggested we donate. I doubt we would have raised nearly as much as we did when the group decided to give.

Perhaps more business leaders should take this approach with their employees. Instead of giving orders, cutting jobs, and hiding challenges, what would happen if they simply asked their teams to suggest solutions?

Make Them Part of the Solution

Five or six years ago, after I gave a speech for the Navy's Women in Leadership Symposium, the folks in charge of the policy office asked me for a meeting to discuss retention issues with junior officers.

During the meeting it quickly became clear that the leadership team had many great ideas for improving retention—increasing funding for dependents to go to college, offering paternity leave, increasing financial assistance with childcare, and providing other perks to reward long-term service.

I was impressed. These leaders recognized their challenges and had lots of great ideas. The only problem was that the sailors also needed to be a part of the solution. The people who would be affected by those decisions needed to have an opportunity to voice their ideas and opinions.

"Your team will likely come up with the exact same list," I suggested to the leadership team. "Maybe not even as many great ideas as you already have...and perhaps some that you never thought of."

"So if they'll come up with the same list, why not just begin implementing?" they asked.

"Because people support that which they help to create, and if they see this as their Navy, and therefore their problem/opportunity, they will do everything they can to help ensure its success."

Over the next few months, we traveled the country, facilitating dialogue with a wide mix of Navy personnel about what the organization could do to retain them. This feedback was used to institute changes, which were communicated through their intranet. After just nine months, turnover of junior officers dropped.

This is the power of involving others in creating solutions.

Bring Them in the Loop

When faced with challenges, few leaders capitalize on the opportunity to ask their team for help. Why? They don't see the opportunity!

Most are too busy watching their own backs to realize that they should be showing their cards—openly discussing their fears and explaining the situation. Doing so increases trust, retention, collaboration, and of course, the bottom line. Being upfront with your team about challenges also gives them the opportunity to help out—to offer ideas and solutions that could lighten your proverbial load.

This kind of vulnerability takes courage. Often leaders neglect to show their cards because they don't want to be seen as incompetent. As a result, they miss out on the credibility they could gain from being honest, open, and human.

When you share your problems with your team and give them an opportunity to be a part of the solution (instead of just cutting their hours and leaving them to fear the worst), they will get creative and driven toward helping you find the best course of action for everyone involved, including the business itself.

They'll come up with ideas you never considered and will be even more committed to the success of your company. Why? Because you will have proven that you're committed to them.

Far beyond simply getting creative ideas that will benefit everyone, these sorts of conversations are at the source of personal accountability, or ownership.

Give Them a Stake

Passionate employees who believe in a company's vision will already feel connected to the brand, and finding ways to make business personal for them will only strengthen their commitment and sense of ownership.

That's why Seth Goldman gives Honest Tea employees who have gone above and beyond the chance to choose barcode numbers for products. As he explained to me, "They can use their birthdays, their children's birthdays, or their anniversary dates. To the consumer it doesn't really make a difference, but it gives employees a sense of ownership in the brand. They can say to other people, 'That's sort of my product, I own that one.'"

His employees feel a greater sense of ownership for their work as a result of this practice. If the code is connected to them in some way, they're naturally going to want the product to do even better.

Dr. Steven J. Kraus, founder and CEO of Future Health Software, takes ownership one step further—putting his money where his mouth is. Years ago he gave 15 percent of his company to his employees, including secretaries and other support staff. "I'm always telling them that everybody matters and that we're all in it together," he told me. "If I'm going to talk the talk, I've got to walk the walk. If everybody matters and everybody is part of this company, then I want them to act like an owner, so I need to make them an owner."

Of course, not every leader can or should give away part of the company, but the smart ones get creative and find their own ways to give their teams a personal stake in the company's success.

CHAPTER 11

Loosen the Reigns

"Planes are safer when the least experienced pilot is flying, because it means the second pilot isn't going to be afraid to speak up."
—Malcolm Gladwell, from *Outliers*

Getting your employees to take ownership means giving them the opportunities and the power to make things happen. In other words, you must give them some degree of autonomy.

Of course, how much autonomy depends on the role, the person, and his or her experience level. Some employees need a little hand-holding, especially when they're new to their positions. But once they've proven themselves capable of doing the work, it's time to loosen the reigns and discover their potential. Otherwise you leave them feeling frustrated and disempowered. And you lose out on the investments you've made in them—either because you're not getting their A-game or because they find other career opportunities where they will be challenged.

Micromanagement Does NOT Provoke Greatness

I met Connie at a coffee shop near my home. After working in the public school system for many years, she recently became principal of a charter school. She was initially hesitant about taking the job, which required an hour-long commute (each way). But after several conversations, the school board convinced her.

How? They promised her autonomy—the opportunity to create a system that worked well by her standards. Connie was sold, which isn't surprising. In fact, 94 percent of employees and 96 percent of HR professionals rate autonomy and independence as either "important" or "very important" aspects of job satisfaction.

Connie started her new job, excited about creating an environment where teachers felt inspired and students excelled. Less than a year later, when she and I spoke, she was looking for a new job.

As it turns out, the school operated on a strict system that had worked well in one charter school and was now being tested in several others. The school board insisted principals follow the manual explicitly. Each class had a script which dictated every word the teachers should say to their students, right down to "Good morning, boys and girls."

Rather than insist her teachers be puppets, Connie refused to discipline them for diverging from their scripts, which only got her into trouble with her employer.

Connie signed up for autonomy but was instead given a prescription for exactly how to do her job. She's a talented leader and a passionate educator, but the school board has put up too many barriers for any principal with experience and vision to succeed. In essence, they have removed the talent from teaching. So Connie—and the quality educators who work for her—have already begun to move into new positions.

Accountability Is Key

Giving your team autonomy is a balancing act. While you don't want to micromanage them into ineffectiveness, you also need to ensure progress gets made toward the vision. The trick to leading autonomous people is setting clear expectations, providing regular feedback, and then holding them accountable for their results.

Getting people to own their results is not always an easy task. It's frustrating when they don't deliver what they say they can or will deliver, or what you know they're capable of delivering. If they're not getting results, your team and your vision suffer.

I had this lesson reinforced for me last year when my partner and I bought a house in Baltimore, Maryland. We decided a splash of paint, a couple ceiling fans, and removing the wet bar from the basement would make this house into our home. So we hired Peter, a contractor, to do the renovations.

Peter came over to get an idea of the work required to complete the job. After a bit of negotiating, we settled on a price. To ensure we were on the same page, I said, "So, I can expect you to do X, Y, and Z for this cost, right?" He agreed. "I'm not a fan of nickel-and-diming," I told him. "So please be sure you are happy with this price." Again, he agreed.

I assumed it was all settled. But on the morning Peter's crew got started, he pulled me aside and said, "Those ceiling fans are going to take a lot of work."

"I'm sure you can handle it," I told him.

"Yeah, but it will take a lot more work to get that room wired for a fan than I thought," he said. "It's going to cost you more."

Filled with anger and frustration, I thought about firing him. Then I considered begging him to do the work at no extra cost. Then I wanted to go yell at the wind. I was mad! I knew this wasn't OK, but I didn't know what to do about it.

After stressing myself out, I finally stopped to think, How do I get this man to honor his word?

"Peter, you had a chance to see my home before you gave me a quote, right?"

"Yes," he said. "But I didn't know the room wasn't wired for the fan. It's going to require more work."

"And whose responsibility is that?" I asked, finally calm(er).

"Mine," he said. "I will take care of it." And he did, without any further discussion.

Holding people to their promises, or even to their greatness, is challenging. It's hard to communicate when a conversation triggers fear—fear of hurting someone's feelings or that they will get mad and do less than their best work. But it's worth the effort to do so.

In the end, Peter went above and beyond what he promised, and my home looked spectacular after his team completed the job.

Trust Your Instincts—and Your People

Nearly every leader I've met has said, "Driven, hard workers are so hard to find." Perhaps this is true. Or perhaps these leaders are micromanaging the motivation right out of their talent.

According to Daniel Pink's research on performance, the three greatest motivators leaders can tap into include:

- Autonomy—The urge to direct our own lives

- Master—The desire to get better and better at something that matters

- Purpose—The yearning to do what we do in the service of something larger than ourselves

In Pink's popular Ted Talk, he explains, "The goal is to get people to take ownership of their work, get creative, and collaborate… People are motivated by autonomy, mastery, and purpose in their work, not by carrots and sticks."

Great leaders trust their instincts and their people. They set expectations and hold their employees accountable for results, but they don't tell them exactly how to do their jobs. They let their teams know what's working and what's not. Then they ask employees for suggestions about how to improve the situation and take risks with them.

David Marquet, a former nuclear submarine commander in the U.S. Navy, learned about the value of autonomy when he was shifted (at the last minute) to command a submarine, which happened to be the newest ship in the fleet. "All the equipment was different," Marquet told me. "I had trained for the wrong submarine, and my crew was trained to do what they were told. And that's a deadly, deadly combination. They were going to do whatever I ordered them to do, but I needed people to think, and that was a totally different approach. If you want people to do stuff, you go around and give orders. You sound confident…like the traditional naval officer in a movie. However, if you want people to think, you do the opposite."

So Marquet swore off giving orders and encouraged his team to think, enabling him to tap into their superior knowledge about the vessel. He gave them the language to come to him with suggestions, rather than waiting around for orders. "They came to me and said, 'Captain, I intend to. I intend to submerge the ship. I intend to start up the reactor. I intend to load a torpedo.' And this fundamentally changed everything about how we operate."

Of course, relinquishing control is hard on any leader, especially one in the military who has been trained to give orders. So Marquet and his team of officers began practicing their new leadership style while off the clock. "We do what we call training your brain," Marquet explained. "So take a friend to coffee. But instead of you ordering your own coffee, turn to your friend and say, 'You order for me. Just pick what you think I want.'"

While a coffee order is certainly not a life-changing decision, Marquet says it's still hard on most people. "As a mammal, you've been programmed over thousands of years to want to be in control, and that's normal. It feels unnatural and scary to give up that control. You're not going to cure yourself of that fear, but it's the leaders who act in the face of that fear and give control to their people anyway who end up achieving amazing things."

Marquet said his officers' reactions to the coffee challenges were amazing. Some people talked about how scary it was, while others were touched that their friends had paid close enough attention to know exactly what they would want. The long-term results of the exercise were also amazing. "I didn't realize it at the time, but I was training them to think like captains," said Marquet. "And then the guys below them started thinking like the department heads, who started thinking like the captains, and the chiefs started thinking like the officers, who were thinking like the department heads...and on and on. So we went from having one leader—one thinker with 134 doers—to having 135 thinking, leading, energetic, engaged, passionate people, and it was a tidal wave. It was total transformation."

Take a cue from Marquet. If you have talented team members, they know how to get results in their areas of expertise as well or better than you do. If some of them don't, maybe it's time to get them the resources or training they need.

HIGHLIGHTS
SECTION 2: OWNERSHIP

1. Take ownership for your beliefs. If you believe your team will underperform, that's what you'll find. But if you believe they'll succeed, you'll have the power to help them do it.

2. When you lead from love—and actually care about the success of your people—you provoke greatness. When you use fear as a motivator, you provoke fear, anxiety, and stress—all of which are toxic for your workplace culture, your customer relations, and your bottom line.

3. Some people have heard encouraging words of affirmation their whole lives; others don't know they're talented and need those around them to help them see their own greatness. Nearly all of us are already A+ performers. The vast majority simply don't know it...yet!

4. People are more dedicated to solving problems when they help to define the solutions. They push harder to accomplish goals they help to create.

5. Most leaders are too busy watching their own backs to realize they should be showing their cards—openly discussing their fears and explaining situations as honestly as they can. Doing so increases trust, retention, collaboration, and of course, the bottom line.

6. Getting your employees to take ownership means giving them opportunities and autonomy. Otherwise you leave them feeling frustrated and disempowered.

Section 3: Intentions

Intentional leaders—regardless of their titles—are magnetic. People want to follow those who set clear expectations, walk with purpose, and include others in their journeys. These behaviors create followership.

Said simply, intentional people intend to achieve worthwhile outcomes, and they intend to pull out the greatness in those around them. They not only clearly understand their values, but they intentionally live in accordance with each of them. When they falter on their values, they don't hesitate to admit, "Oops, that was not my intention," and then course-correct.

While most leaders say, "I intend to get them to do what I want them to do," those who provoke greatness ask, "Who am I being that is (or is not) causing those around me to be great?" When your intentions are to benefit everyone involved, you stand a far greater chance of reaching the outcomes you desire—and a far greater chance of provoking greatness.

Those who provoke greatness are intentional about their decisions and communication. They are particularly deliberate when it comes to:

- **Vision**: Why are you in this business? What will be different because of the work you're doing? What do you stand for and believe in? (We already covered this in Section 1, but it's important enough to bear repeating.)

- **Values**: What does your company/team currently value? What values are you committed to demonstrating?

- **Culture**: What type of environment will enable you and your team to flourish? What type of culture will attract and nourish people who believe in what you believe in?

- **Growth**: How do you want to grow your company and what are you unwilling to sacrifice to achieve that growth, particularly as it relates to your values and culture?

- **Employee Development**: What's important to each of your employees? What are their dreams and how can you help them achieve their goals?

We'll examine each of these interconnected elements throughout this section.

CHAPTER 12

Do You Know What You Value?

"Your beliefs become your thoughts,
Your thoughts become your words,
Your words become your actions,
Your actions become your habits,
Your habits become your values,
Your values become your destiny."

—Mahatma Gandhi

Understanding your intentions helps clarify what you really value. Every person has values, and so does every company. Those values speak volumes about who they are and what they're striving to achieve. The problem is that many leaders don't act in accordance with what they say they value. Still others don't know what they value. But their employees and customers do, because we all communicate what's important to us every day, whether or not we're aware of doing so.

Dr. Freeman Hrabowski—president of University of Maryland (Baltimore County) and one of Time magazine's "Most Influential People in the World" in 2012—puts it well. He says values are among the most important aspects of leadership, and "at the heart of those values must be integrity and authenticity, because if people believe you are sincere in what you are doing as a leader, they will give you a chance to succeed. But if people don't trust you, it's very difficult to make sustainable progress."

If you're not intentional about your values—both identifying them and living them—you risk losing the trust of your team and your customers, and eventually losing your best employees.

Your Reputation Is on the Line

Shaun Callahan is a passionate, music-loving "people person" with strong connections in Baltimore, Maryland. He is fun, creative, highly talented, and dedicated to excellence.

After several years in corporate sales, he saw an ad for a job selling custom music compilations to companies in Baltimore. Perfect, he thought. I can leverage my passion for music and my local network.

Rather than submit a traditional résumé, Shaun made a CD with his voice (over background music) describing his passion for music, his connections in the community, and his experience in sales. Then he added an additional hour of songs he felt accurately portrayed him.

It was remarkable, and he was hired.

Soon after joining the company, Shaun discovered the sales position was more of an account executive position. This wasn't what he wanted, but he stuck it out for several months and finally got his opportunity to pitch clients. Not surprisingly, he landed his first big contract within days—a retailer who wanted custom music for the grand opening of his new store.

To ensure the client received the music on time, Shaun followed up with his colleagues, only to discover the company had more contracts than they could fulfill. Realizing his reputation was associated with this sale, and knowing the company would not fulfill his promise, Shaun spent the next several hours pulling together a playlist. He personally delivered the music to the client, along with the equipment necessary to ensure good sound quality. Then he turned in his letter of resignation and started Pep Video—his own business cutting pre-recorded videos (another of his passions).

Shaun is the epitome of integrity, hard work, discipline, and honesty. He knows the company he keeps—and the company he works for—says something about him. So he wants it to say something good.

I'm sure Shaun's former employers would say they also value integrity, hard work, discipline, and honesty. But they failed to demonstrate these values. And as we all know, actions speak louder than words.

Perhaps that's why more than 40 percent of people don't respect the person to whom they report. And more than 50 percent say they have different values than their employers.

If you want the respect of your team, your customers, and your community, you have to go beyond declaring your values; you must live them.

What Do You Value?

Some experts insist leaders need to clearly define five to seven core values for their companies, communicate them clearly, and behave in accordance with them. Many do just that...or at least the first part. They create a list of values that sound good, put them on a plaque on the wall, include them in the company handbook, and never really think about them again.

Big mistake! Not only do a leader's values reflect on the company. Values also drive internal culture and define how employees treat each other.

Capital One CEO Rich Fairbank puts it best:

❝❝ As a leader, the most important thing is not what you articulate about the culture; it's the behaviors and the values that you show. That drives what gets rewarded, who gets ahead, and the choices that are made. People watch the values a leader shows and adapt to it. So many companies have these beautiful culture statements that hang on the wall, but the CEO is a living violation of that, and then it's a negative value. I mean, it's laughable to display your values on the wall and then not live them.

If you're not living and working by your values, your team will quickly realize it and ignore them altogether. The better strategy is to intentionally highlight your company values based on the following questions:

- What outcomes do I want to achieve?
- What are the qualities I want to see in the people I hire?

When you know the answers to these questions, you can identify and focus on the values that will help you achieve your desired results and then create an environment that attracts people who share those values.

What Do They Value?

Employees who share a company's values naturally want to work harder to help those companies achieve higher levels of excellence. That's why the most effective values are co-created by the team, based on collective agreement about what's most important to ensure successful working relationships.

Once you have a list of values you think are important and relevant to the vision, let your team help you narrow it down. From there, it's a matter of continuing to keep the values fresh through communication and purposeful action. Remember, unless you're actually living your values, your team won't live them either.

Now, What Do You REALLY Value?

Often what we say we value and what we act as though we value are two different things. That's why it's important to gain clarity about what's actually showing up. When you know what you're acting as though you value, you can make adjustments based on the values you want to exude.

To discover the values you're currently living, ask yourself the following questions at the end of each day:

- How did you spend your time today? (This reveals what you're really prioritizing.)

- Did you honor all of your commitments? (If so, you probably value honesty, integrity, and dependability.)

- Did you learn something new about your employees? How about your clients? (If so, you probably value your people.)

- Did you exercise, eat healthily, and practice meditation, or some other form of spirituality? (If so, you probably value health.)

- Did you take care to ensure you had energy left at the end of the day for your family? (If so, you probably value family.)

- Did you read or learn something new? (If so, you probably value learning, growth, and innovation.)

- Did you share what you learned with those around you? (If so, you probably value collaboration.)

If there are certain values you think you have or want to have, ask yourself how you lived out—or betrayed—those values each day.

For more on defining and living your values, visit www.MeasurableGreatness.com/HowToProvoke.

CHAPTER 13
Culture Killers

"I've learned that people will forget what you said, people will forget what you did, but people will never forget how you made them feel."
—Maya Angelou

When you declare your values and are intentional about behaving in accordance with them, you create an intentional culture—for your team and every person who interacts with your organization.

A company's culture reveals many truths about the people who lead it. When leaders are not intentional about their values, or choose values that work against their employees, their customers, or their visions, it shows up in their corporate culture. This lack of intentionality comes with a price tag. Not only does it hurt productivity and the bottom line; it leads to retention problems and a poor reputation with customers.

The best measure of your core values is whether, after interacting with you, an employee would recommend your company. Think about that for a minute; if the people on your team don't encourage their friends and family to get involved by either buying your products or joining your team, what does that say about your company culture? Time on the job, money earned, or the facts of the case are irrelevant. The feelings you evoke are what matter most. Eliciting positive feelings takes humanity, vulnerability, and connection, not more cash or perks.

How do you know if your culture—and the values that define your culture—are provoking productive feelings? Here are three sure signs your values need shifting:

- Your team thinks you're selfish.
- Your team doesn't trust you.
- Your people don't treat one another with respect.

Your Team Thinks You're Selfish

A corporate culture built around envy and self-centeredness might create short-term success, but without passionate employees who believe in the vision, that success won't be sustainable.

In a recent conversation with my friends Greg and Kathy about their experiences with previous employers, Greg told us, "These guys start technology companies, sell them, and then just leave everyone to fend for themselves. The last guy I worked for actually sold the company and then sent out an email asking the team what fancy car he should buy. Bonuses for his employees would have been nice."

Kathy nodded and said, "That happens in this industry all the time. I've been lucky. The guys who started the last company I worked for had an experience like that, so they didn't repeat the same mistakes. We got bonuses every time our product hit new levels of success."

Then Kathy told us about the bad experience that made her previous employers so generous. Apparently the day their former boss sold his company, he called the office from his car phone (this was back in the '80s, when car phones were a luxury) and fired everyone.

As Greg and Kathy talked about the companies they'd worked for and the people who ran them, I couldn't help but wonder if these leaders know the kind of stories being told about them. Kathy's positive words about her previous employer were both inspiring and captivating. I won't soon forget their names or the companies they built. Likewise, I won't forget the players in Greg's stories.

Which of these leaders do you think will attract and retain the most dedicated, talented team players in their next venture? The self-absorbed man who had the audacity to boast about his greediness, or the generous leaders who shared the credit (and the profits) with their team? I certainly know which company I'd want to work for—and which one I'd warn people to avoid.

If your interest is bigger than making a quick buck in the short term, consider what kind of environment naturally elicits a desire to dream and act big. Nothing remarkable ever happens overnight; great accomplishments take decision, commitment, consistency, and collaboration. What does your team environment elicit right now?

Your Team Doesn't Trust You

Intentional leaders are open and honest about what's needed to achieve their goals and the vision, and about any challenges that might stand in the way. They communicate clearly and in a timely manner so people have the information they need to do their very best work. In doing so, they create a culture where people trust each other enough to share openly and to collaborate.

The problem is that most leaders would rather have a root canal than a one-on-one meeting with an employee to discuss what's going well and what needs improvement—or how the company is doing and what the team needs to do to move the ball forward.

For many leaders, communication can be challenging and even a bit intimidating. Being honest with someone, especially when the truth isn't pleasant, feels uncomfortable and risky. They worry about the perceived consequences of what is shared. Often they lack clarity about what needs to be shared or how to deal with the response or questions. They don't fully understand what they want to say, so rather than thinking it out, they simply remain silent.

In a recent meeting with eight CEOs, one leader literally squirmed in his seat when we began talking about the importance of sharing our passions every day. It's easier—and less risky—to hang out in your office, keep your head focused on reaching numbers, and respond to emails, than it is to get out in front of your team and share your passion, commitment, and challenges.

Such sharing leaves us vulnerable, and that's not comfortable territory for most of us. We worry: What if they see that I don't have a clue? What if I don't lead them to reaching this vision? What if I fail to reach the goal I intended? Or worse yet, what if the company folds because I didn't make this work?

Years ago I worked with a vice president whose department hadn't reached its numbers for three years. Long story short: He needed to have a conversation with his team and acknowledge that he was failing to inspire and engage them. Doing so would put the onus on him and provide fertile ground for fresh ideas to emerge.

He had the meeting and told them: "I have been in this position for three years. My job is to lead this team to reaching our quota. My job is not to bring in all the funds myself. It's to help you reach your goals. And I haven't. At least not yet. It recently occurred to me that I cannot do it without you. We need to work together to reach this goal, and I'd like your input on what changes are necessary to have our team exceed quota in the next three months."

Then he listened, took notes, asked them to take responsibility for their ideas, and began supporting them in achieving their goals. In less than six months, they greatly exceeded quota for the year.

When leaders are intentional about their communication—when their teams know what's happening, why it's happening, how they will be impacted, and how they can help—people are much more likely to remain focused on the vision.

Granted, such transparency is not always possible or even legal. Announcing some information—such as pending mergers or acquisitions, or certain financial data—might even be prohibited by nondisclosure agreements or SEC guidelines. The key is to be as honest and share as much information as you can.

Your People Don't Treat One Another with Respect

Another way to gauge the effectiveness of your culture is to observe how your employees treat each other.

During a shopping trip with my friend Amy, we popped into a specialty-clothing store. As we browsed the merchandise, I couldn't help but overhear a conversation between one of the sales clerks and her manager.

With almost a sense of desperation, the sales clerk asked, "When can I take a break?"

At first her manager ignored her. When the clerk repeated her question, the manager responded, "You'll go on break when I tell you to go on break."

I felt like saying, "I'm right here. I heard that." I was standing just a couple feet away from them.

Perhaps they were functioning with less staff than they needed, so the manager was particularly stressed out. Or perhaps the lady asking for a break was just a chronic whiner, and the manager was tired of hearing it. But the reasons for this nastiness simply didn't matter to me. I walked out without buying anything, because I refuse to support a company where people are treated that way.

Turns out, I'm not the only one. Research shows that people are less likely to buy from a company when an employee is rude, either to them or other employees. Kindness really does matter— not only for retaining productive employees, but also for retaining customers.

Unfortunately rudeness in the workplace is on the rise. Over the past 14 years, 98 percent of workers have reported experiencing uncivil behavior. In 2011, half were treated rudely at least once a week—a quarter of the number who said the same thing in 1998.

Rude, disrespectful treatment of employees rarely starts with the manager; it comes from a lack of strong values in the company's culture, which is a direct reflection of the CEO's values.

CHAPTER 14

The Intentional Culture

"To win in the marketplace, you must first win in the workplace."
—Doug Conant

When it comes to company culture, the goal is to create an environment in which people enjoy coming to work—where there is a palpable sense of passion, where people don't bicker or compete because they're too busy collaborating and bringing the vision to life.

This is hard for leaders who are accustomed to telling people what to do and promoting top-down, command-and-control environments. As a result, we end up seeing organizations buy awards, campaign to have their names included on lists of top companies to work for, market their culture, create mentoring programs, and push for positive pronouncements on social media.

A shelf full of "best company to work for" trophies might create traction to your company, but if you're not putting your money—and energy—where your mouth is, people won't be fooled for long, and they will soon seek employment with companies that genuinely have great cultures.

A phenomenal workplace culture isn't something you buy or campaign for. And it's far too important to leave to chance. As John Taft, CEO of RBC Wealth Management, puts it:

Culture is everything when it comes to responsible, long-term business success. Culture is what exists before any given leader shows up, and it's what exists after any given leader moves on. Culture is in the DNA of an organization. It is not something that a leader necessarily goes out and creates. A leader's job is to discover, communicate, and reinforce culture. If you don't get culture right, nothing else matters.

Something to Brag About

Smart leaders are realizing they have to intentionally build, not buy, their cultures—making their companies something people decide to brag about. Some are so good at building these communities that they leave employees wanting to share about their experiences.

Several years ago, Honest Tea was still a fairly small business with limited financial resources. Still, when one employee's son had a terrible accident and needed $10,000 to fly halfway across the country for medical treatment, the company's founders were quick to show just how much they cared.

Debra Schwartz, Honest Tea's vice president of human resources, told me the story:

> ❝ The employee asked us to loan her the money and promised to repay the company. We threw the corporate credit card down, no questions asked. It took three years for her to pay us back, but we were just happy to be able to help and show her we were there for her. When employees are going through difficult times (and even during good times), it's our job to nourish them as people—to show them we are just as committed to them as they are to us. The human aspect of human resources is the most important part.

While it's certainly not unheard of for a company to help out an employee facing a life-or-death crisis, what made this situation remarkable is that the executives didn't tell anyone. No one picked up the phone to alert the press. They didn't boast about their altruism to employees or customers. When the story finally broke, it was because the employee started telling her colleagues—and eventually the media—what the company did for her.

These leaders' intention was to help their employee, not to get kudos for it. In the end, the company got both, which is often the outcome of treating people well and doing good deeds. After all, what goes around does usually come back around.

As John Mackey and Raj Sisodia write in *Conscious Capitalism*:

> **❝** Conscious businesses do what is right because they believe it is right. They treat all their stakeholders well because that is the right, humane, and sensible thing to do—and because it is also smart business practice to do so. They operate with a sense of higher purpose because that is what gets their people excited about coming to work. The leaders of conscious businesses care about service to others because that is ultimately what leads to fulfillment and value creation.

If Honest Tea's leaders had focused on getting good publicity for helping a team member, rather than living up to their values as an honest and caring company, the effect would not have been the same.

Putting Them First

Disney is another excellent example of a company with an intentional culture. Understanding that talented, high-achieving people tend to get bored and want to continue developing themselves and elevating their careers, Disney encourages employees to seek out career advancement, even if they need to go elsewhere. The reasoning is very simple: If the company's leaders support their people, people will support them. In other words, if they encourage individual achievement, individuals will achieve great things for them. As a result, many employees leave the company, go out and get more experience, and then return to Disney—bringing all their new skills, resources, and connections with them. These people also tell their friends and family about their experiences, which leads to more talented people seeking opportunities at Disney.

Is Disney perfect? Of course not. "Perfect" doesn't exist. But Disney's leaders are intentional, and they continually refine their processes based on the intentions they've established.

Thanks to the leadership of Cheryl Sandberg, chief operating officer of Facebook, the company instituted "pregnancy parking" for employees, and offers paid maternity and paternity leave. Zappos encourages employees to take their time with each customer and to be themselves—human beings, not just robots who read from scripts.

These are just a few of the forward-thinking leaders and innovative companies that get intentional about culture, and reap the rewards.

Creating an Intentional Culture

Whether or not you're intentional about creating culture, one will be created. It's simply what happens when human beings share space and goals. So unless you're launching a brand new company or unit, you're not starting from scratch.

Shifting an ineffective culture is much more difficult than intentionally creating a brand new one, but it's absolutely possible. Use the following questions to evaluate what isn't working in your current culture and determine what needs to change:

- What values are currently being demonstrated in our workplace?

- Is morale low? Do people turn in half-hearted work and bicker with their colleagues?

- What new habits does the leadership team need to begin demonstrating that will cause others to shift their behaviors?

- What really matters to people looking for employment?

- How can we create an environment that fosters their success?

- Why would they want to stay here?

- Why would they want to work hard and think big?

- How can we ensure we've created the best work environment, based on their desires?

For more on how to evaluate and shift a broken culture, visit www.MeasurableGreatness.com/HowToProvoke.

CHAPTER 15

Will Growth Kill Your Culture?

"A business has to be involving, it has to be fun, and it has to exercise your creative instincts."

—Richard Branson

Culture is easier to create within a small company, especially when you're the entrepreneur. In fact, to some degree, the team that helps you launch helps you create your culture.

The challenge is that the larger a business grows, and the more cooks you get in the kitchen, the harder it can be to keep your company's culture strong. People start to feel more like cogs in a wheel than key drivers of the company's vision and mission. Processes start to take the place of the creativity that once fueled the team's passion and energy. And suddenly the team—people who once thought they could change the world—dread coming to work every day.

It doesn't have to be this way! The key is to be intentional about how you grow, and to protect the vision, values, culture, and people who helped the company become successful in the first place.

Don't Drink the Kool-Aid...
When I had lunch with Sam, a new friend and talented salesman, I was captivated by the story of how he went from breaking company records to looking for a new opportunity.

A few years out of college, Sam was working in sales for a fast-growing new software company. According to him, the culture was pretty stereotypical of the dot-com startup—with foosball tables, refrigerators stocked with beer, Friday happy hours, casual work attire, etc. As Sam put it, "It was the perfect job for a single person in his mid-20s."

Sam quickly earned the respect of the company's leadership team, who not only listened to his ideas, but also implemented them. If fact, they regularly told him, "Someday we'll be working for you."

Sam enjoyed his work so much that he spent all his free time thinking about how to contribute to the company, beyond just hitting sales numbers. "I prided myself on being more than a quota," he told me. "I felt like a thought leader and an innovator. And for the first few years, I was treated as such."

Thanks to innovators like Sam, the business grew quickly, and the founders eventually decided to take the company public. None of the executives had done this before, so they added some "seasoned" veterans to the management team—people who had worked with companies during such transitions. To make the business seem like a legitimate, publically-traded company, these new managers implemented some dramatic changes, including what Sam called "overly-corrective policies and general bureaucracy that would make government employees scratch their heads."

While I'm sure these folks meant well, they didn't realize the culture and employees are what made the company successful. The shift in culture resulted in unhappy employees, and most of the high-achievers simply left.

Over the next few years, as the company added more levels of management, the disconnect between corporate culture and employee morale grew. "The tipping point came when a large private-equity firm acquired the company," Sam told me. "They radically altered it from a high-growth, top-line-focused business to one where only the bottom line mattered. Now our corporate culture is marked by a sense of hopelessness, instead of the optimism and innovation that once fueled our growth."

Like many of his remaining colleagues, Sam started looking for a job where his innovative ideas and passion could be put to good use. As he put it, "I am simply wasting my brain power here."

Sam told me he doesn't believe the problem lies in what or how this happened. "Many companies go public and/or get acquired without changing the culture or employee morale," he said. "But things go south when companies forget to focus on the why (the vision) and the who (the people who made the company successful)."

Less than a year after sharing this story with me, Sam landed a job in a company where innovation is not only encouraged; it's expected. Three months into his new position, he shared his top three innovative ideas with his boss and got the green light to pursue one of them.

...Drink the Tea Instead

Sam is absolutely right about corporate growth. Companies grow, go public, and get acquired all the time. While many of them do so at the expense of what originally made them successful, smart leaders know that intentionally great cultures are to be treasured, not toyed with. The value is inherent in the culture, not the widget the company sells. Every company sells widgets; few create great cultures.

When Seth Goldman co-founded Honest Tea in 1998, he was a man on a mission—with an inspiring vision for how his product could impact the health of consumers, and strong values that attracted equally passionate people who helped him make his small business great. Now the company is the nation's top-selling ready-to-drink, organic bottled tea and is carried in more than 100,000 outlets.

When The Coca-Cola Company purchased Honest Tea in 2011, keeping Goldman's leadership team in place, employees worried the acquisition would change the culture they loved and that many of them had helped to create. Debra Schwartz, Honest Tea's vice president of human resources, told me:

> ❝ When we were going through the acquisition, it was hard for us. There was a period of time where I felt like I was banging my head against the wall. Everyone was up in arms and scared for their jobs. They trusted us, but they didn't understand what the change would

mean. Seth and I kept telling them we weren't going to have layoffs or combine roles, but it just took time for us to prove that we were going to keep sticking to our values and that we would protect our culture.

How did they prove it? By not letting the things that mattered—the intentional steps they'd taken to create a fantastic culture—change. For example, one of the company's values is (no big shocker here) honesty. So the company has always had a monthly call for all employees, where each manager summarizes everything that's happening in his or her department—the good, the bad, and the ugly—and the CFO shares all the company's financials. "We were just as transparent throughout the acquisition," said Schwartz. "We were upfront about any changes that would or wouldn't be happening. At no point did we withhold information or refuse to answer questions."

Under Goldman and Schwartz's leadership, Honest Tea has always valued its people, making extra efforts to ensure they feel appreciated and cared for—from providing them with healthy snack packs, to creating "Afternoon Tea" (a daily newsletter with updates about the company as well as employee birthdays, weddings, child births, and other big personal news), to sending handwritten birthday cards to employees. These traditions have been kept alive, despite the company's growth and acquisition.

"This was really key to keeping our team engaged and passionate about the company," said Schwartz. "The longer these things didn't change, the more people said, 'I guess we really are going to be OK.' That's the thing. If you take care of your employees, they'll take care of your business. Sometimes people think that taking care of your employees is just financial. That's not true. Sometimes it's emotional."

The result of these efforts: a 93 percent retention rate since The Coca-Cola Company purchased Honest Tea, and a team of people who still love coming to work.

"When we surveyed our team in 2012, while were going through the acquisition, 89 percent of employees said it was a great place to work," said Schwartz. "In 2013, once they realized we were definitely staying the course and still dedicated to them and our original mission, it was 92 percent. That means a lot to us."

It also means they're doing something right. As further proof of Honest Tea's powerful culture, Schwartz told me about the vice president of operations, Ed Castro, who came from the same role at Pepsi. When Castro first started at Honest Tea, he wore a suit every day and was very process-oriented, as opposed to Goldman, in his shorts and plaid shirts and with his very entrepreneurial leadership style. It took Castro about nine months to "drink the tea," but soon he was coming to work in jeans and sneakers, and before long, he had a tattoo of the company's green dragon logo on his chest. "He realized we all meant what we said," Schwartz explained. "We believed in this—in what we were doing and everything we said we believed in. And soon he was believing too."

That's what happens when you combine a strong vision with clear values, and then create a culture that is (as Schwartz put it) "contagious." People flock to it. They start to "drink the tea." They become passionate about the vision. They care about the future of your company and helping it grow and become great, because they know you care about helping them grow into greatness right along with you.

CHAPTER 16

The Thing About Feedback

"A leader's role is to raise people's aspirations for what they can become and to release their energies so they will try to get there."

—David Gergen

Intentional leaders are quick to provide feedback—in the right time and in the right way. They don't wait until annual reviews to let employees know how they're measuring up. Because they intend to provoke greatness, they make it their job to do so every single day.

Without feedback it's nearly impossible to improve, and lack of improvement leads to disengagement. Managers who give little or no feedback to their teams fail to engage 98 percent of them. That's an awful lot of people showing up to work who would rather be anywhere else.

Despite the importance of feedback, it's not an easy thing for most of us. Some worry about inflating egos, while others fear destroying self-esteem. Still others are "too busy" to worry about such things as employee development (you know, leadership). And many simply don't know how to do it effectively.

Don't Confuse Motivation with Manipulation

The key to effective feedback lies in our intentions, not our methods. If your intention is to judge or criticize, to be right, or to show them how stupid they are, you'll fail to inspire a shift in their behavior. The intention of feedback must be to help the other person reach his or her goals, and to help the company reach its vision. Otherwise people will see straight through your inauthentic efforts, and your feedback will be wasted breath.

In December 2012, I had this lesson driven home for me. With a clear vision for increasing community in my office building, I set out to inspire the person responsible for planning events, a woman named Sahara, who always looked angry.

My first inspiration strategy was complimenting her. "Do you know how wonderful you are?" I asked. "Your smile is magnificent. Keep using it."

"Really?" she responded, beaming. "Me?"

I thought I was golden! Now I could influence her to do what I wanted—help me get to know my suitemates.

Wrong! The smile lasted about 20 minutes and did nothing in the way of inspiring her to plan an event. So I started asking questions about her job satisfaction and challenges. Then I told her how to get more opportunities at work and get better results with her leadership team.

When she did nothing with my advice, I got irritated. All this effort for nothing? Sitting in my office in disbelief, I could not understand why someone who speaks and writes about inspiration for a living could get nothing more out of this woman than a short-lived smile.

Then it hit me: I had confused manipulation with motivation.

A couple days later, I asked Sahara, "How's your career going? Do you like what you do?"

"No," she said. "I'd rather be in human resources. I got my degree in HR, and I'd like to find a job in that industry."

No wonder my efforts to motivate her fell short; I knew nothing about what was motivating her. Turns out, she couldn't care less about community events and only took the position to cover her bills until she could find something that better suited her interests and passions. So I started listening to what she wanted for her career, making appropriate connections, and providing a bit of guidance for these introductions. Her attitude toward my advice shifted immediately.

When my intention was to manipulate her into doing what I wanted (planning community events), she did nothing I suggested. When my intention was to help her get what was important to her (a job she wanted), she got into action.

To provoke greatness in others, your intentions must be about helping them, not just yourself. People instinctively know the difference between someone who wants something from them, and someone who wants great things for them. And guess which person they'll work hard for.

Before you provide feedback, ask yourself: Is this feedback valuable to this person's professional/personal growth? If it's not, consider what kind of feedback would be helpful.

Don't Forget the Power of Praise

The vast majority of us were never shown how to appreciate and validate others, for fear of giving them a "big head."

As Tony Schwartz, president and CEO of the Energy Project, puts it, "We're not fluent in the language of positive emotions in the workplace. We're so unaccustomed to sharing them that we don't feel comfortable doing so. Heartfelt appreciation is a muscle we've not spent much time building, or felt encouraged to build."

Yet research shows that when used correctly, praise is an incredibly effective tool for motivating employees and provoking greatness. Managers who focus on employee strengths are 30 times more likely to manage actively engaged workers than managers who deny feedback. And companies that effectively appreciate employees and leave them feeling valued receive a return on equity and assets more than triple that experienced by other firms.

Talk about making the case for kindness!

Some people understand the value of praise better than others. Over a recent dinner with Jim Young, a sales manager for Google, I listened closely as he told about the system his company has in place to acknowledge team members who go above and beyond for customers.

Jim explained. "For example, if someone drives several hours and stays longer to ensure the job gets done, I submit a form that specifically articulates what the person did and why I think it's worthy of a cash reward. Within 24 hours, an executive has accepted my request to reward the staff member, and a check is cut immediately."

"Wow!" I said. "How many of these small checks have you cashed?"

His response was so wise and inspiring that it has stayed with me: "I've received my fair share, but I've given far more than I've received."

What if we all took Jim's approach to feedback? What if instead of asking, "Don't they see how hard I work?" we asked, "Who is really doing a great job, and how can I acknowledge them for their efforts?"

What if the old adage that "you get what you give" is true? Would you consider giving other people the very thing most of us want more of—a few kind words and recognition for their successes, regardless of your position or theirs? Maybe instead of saying, "I want them to work harder," you'd say, "I'm going to work harder at acknowledging them."

Imagine how much different the business world would be if every leader—and every employee—started thinking that way, and made an intentional effort to not only point out when their people have room to grow, but also when they've done great work.

Don't Say It if You Don't Mean It

Appreciation means feeling grateful. If you're not really feeling it, don't say it. People can sense when you're being authentic and when your words stem from an ulterior motive.

I used to believe there was no such thing as over-appreciating someone, or at least, I could not have told you what "overdone" appreciation looked like. Then about a year ago, I started attending a new networking group, where I met Janet.

The first time we spoke, Janet pointed at me and announced to the entire group, "This one is special." Obviously I relished the glow of her warm words. But over the course of the meeting, she said the same things about me at least half a dozen times. I was new to the group, so I overlooked my increasing discomfort and thanked her for each compliment.

The next time I crossed paths with Janet, she kindly introduced me to another dozen people, again telling each one how extraordinary I am. About halfway through that networking function, her compliments started to feel inauthentic, and I began to wonder what she wanted from me. Sure enough, she approached with me a "business opportunity"—or better said, an opportunity for her to grow her income by recruiting me to sell products under her (i.e., a pyramid scheme).

Some leaders give inauthentic praise, not because they have manipulative intentions, but simply because they've heard that praising people is motivational, so they feel the need to be a cheerleader all the time. But those good intentions can backfire. While people want to feel appreciated and hear they're doing a good job, constantly validating people, rather than reserving praise for moments when you're genuinely impressed, encourages them to be inauthentic. And most people—particularly those who take pride in their work—can spot phoniness a mile away, making the unearned praise a source of irritation, not inspiration.

My friend Jacob interned with a non-profit organization where he had a boss who constantly praised average work. While this leader was probably trying to boost morale, his style had the opposite effect on Jacob. "My motivation went through the floor, because simply showing up and putting my butt in the seat was considered miraculous," he told me. "The only thing worse than not being recognized for excellent work is being praised for mediocre work."

Get Specific

"Thank you" is a very powerful phrase. But to ensure those words don't lose their impact, get specific. For example, you could say something like, "I really enjoy watching you lead Jeff; it's clear he feels empowered by your mentoring," or "You've got some mad skills with Excel, and I really appreciate you producing such a valuable slide for my meeting," or "Your passion for writing really shines through in your work. I'm grateful to have you on my team."

Before you give praise, ask yourself what—specifically—this person did to prompt your kind words. I recently practiced this very skill with a waitress. When I heard myself say, "Thank you for being so great," I realized that wasn't very specific. So I added, "Your passion for food, combined with your natural conversational abilities, is remarkable." She walked away holding her shoulders a little higher, and I got a chance to practice giving specific and authentic feedback.

Ask yourself what specific qualities your employees consistently demonstrate that deserve acknowledgement. If you cannot find anything, look deeper. Also how do those skills, talents, or efforts contribute to the company's vision and/or bottom line? When you can tie positive feedback into to a sense of purpose, it's even more powerful.

Consider the Individual

Some people love to receive public praise—to be bragged about in front of others or to have their contributions recognized in a company press release or newsletter. But others might be embarrassed by such attention and would prefer a private conversation, email, or even text message. While I cannot say I understand shying away from public praise, I've seen enough people get embarrassed that I now pause and consider the individual before saying anything.

Given what you know about each of your team members, what would be the best way to recognize/praise each of them? (Hint: If you don't know which of your employees are shy and which are glory junkies, you might want to spend a little more time getting to know them.)

Just as importantly, what is the best way to give them constructive feedback—based on their experience levels, personalities, and aptitudes? Research shows that people who consider themselves experts are more eager to hear negative feedback, while novices tend to seek out positive responses. The reason is simple: Experienced employees feel more confident about their skills and don't need as many pep talks; they just want to know how they can be even better. Newbies tend to need positive reinforcement while they figure out how to be successful. Too much "constructive criticism" can be discouraging for them.

Bottom line: The better you know your employees, the better your feedback will be received.

CHAPTER 17

How Do YOU Think You're Doing?

"A leader is best when people barely know he exists, when his work is done, his aim fulfilled, they will say: we did it ourselves."

—Lao Tzu

Feedback is clearly important. However, there's a big difference between providing productive feedback and providing constant validation and praise for everything from performing basic job functions to simply showing up for work.

On a recent flight, I struck up a conversation with my seat-mate Leah, who was putting together a presentation entitled "Creating a Coaching Culture." After learning more about her project, I shared a bit about my work with generational diversity and executive coaching.

"Our seasoned professionals have got to learn how to give a great deal more feedback," Leah told me. "Young professionals grew up getting trophies just for being on teams, whether they were any good or not, and they're used to receiving constant feedback on everything they do."

Having heard that very idea expressed a billion times over the past decade, and even having said so myself, I couldn't quite figure out why it seemed so wrong in the moment. It's certainly true that Millennials got trophies just for being on teams, and that they thrive on feedback as a form of encouragement. But is training seasoned professionals to provide constant validation really the best solution to the problem?

No. That is, unless you want to suck the life out of your team!

Ask the Right Questions

Is there a way leaders can teach their employees, across generations, to give themselves a bit of validation and reassurance—leaving them feeling empowered, rather than needy? Absolutely.

Most people already know how they're doing, even if they don't acknowledge it. If this is true, then perhaps the answer lies in providing the right questions, rather than the right feedback. While you don't want to miss an opportunity to praise those who have gone above and beyond, you can also teach employees to regularly evaluate themselves. Simply ask the right open-ended questions and let them find their own answers.

These questions might include:

- What do you enjoy most about your career so far? What's not working so well, and why?

- In what ways/areas are you doing very well?

- How can you step up your game?

- What experiences and/or skills would you like to gain, and how can you create opportunities for yourself?

- If you could do any job, what would it be?

- What do you like most about your job?

- What do you like most about our company?

- What would you like to be doing more of, and how can I help you?

- What's most important to you in your career?

- Where would you love to be in five years? Why?

These questions aren't in any particular order, and none of them will work the same way with every person. Pick the ones that resonate most with your style and that seem most appropriate for your employees. If you know the people on your team, you'll have a good idea what's appropriate for each individual.

Keep 'Em Coming

The more questions you ask, the more you'll understand what inspires and drives your team. More importantly, they'll get to know themselves better. And isn't the end-goal of great leadership to create other leaders—people who know what they want, how to achieve it, and how to help others do the same?

Not only will this strategy save you the time and energy needed to pat everyone on the back all the time, but it will also allow them access to their own validation. And there's no more powerful or important validation than our own.

Of course, you have to do more than simply ask questions to create a powerful conversation and leadership opportunity. An authentic desire to hear the answer is where the power lies. Stay connected and check in with them on a regular basis so you have more opportunities to ask questions, and so you know when problems arise and when celebrations are deserved.

When you provoke your team to reach beyond what they ever thought possible, they will rise.

CHAPTER 18

Who's Provoking YOUR Greatness?

"It is the province of knowledge to speak. And it is the privilege of wisdom to listen."

—Oliver Wendell Holmes

Just over a year ago, I started taking voice lessons. My mother was a vocalist, and I've always wondered whether I had the same talent. Having never taken a single lesson (with the exception of music class in elementary school), I hired an instructor and started with the basics.

To keep myself engaged, I chose a song that inspires me: "Amazing Grace." In retrospect it was probably not the best song for a beginner. But despite its difficulty, the lyrics always leave me feeling uplifted.

I recorded my instructor singing the song so I could use it to practice. The problem was that I could not hear my pitch; I didn't know if the sound coming out of my mouth matched the sound emanating from my recorder.

So I practiced in the most acoustically sound room in my home: my shower. With its big glass door, fully surrounded by walls and ceiling, the echo effect was perfect. I could finally hear myself. And after a few weeks, my voice sounded just like the one on the tape...or so I thought.

Too supportive to provide real feedback, my partner Yvette shared encouraging words like, "Keep working at it; you'll get it."

My cat, on the other hand, was much more honest with me. At first I truly thought Everest was sending me loving, supportive energy as she sat outside the glass door and tried to imitate my sound. Her voice sounded more like a high-pitched screech than singing. But hey, she's only a cat.

Every time I went into the shower to practice, she'd sit outside the door and meow. How cute, I thought. I love you too, sweet kitty. It wasn't until I finally listened to a recording of myself that I realized I sounded more like Everest than I thought. Yikes!

As I have continued to work at the basics, she no longer screeches at me, but the experience left me wondering how many times I've been given valuable feedback and refused to recognize it as such—instead hearing what I wanted to hear.

Recognize Feedback When You See It

We're always receiving feedback—good and bad—but not always in words. Often the feedback is in the results we're getting…or not getting.

If you don't get picked for a promotion, that's feedback. It's not very specific, but it's certainly feedback. When your team is complacent, fails to share information, and doesn't complete work on time, that's valuable feedback about your leadership style. On the other hand, when your team is fully engaged and enthusiastic, refers their friends and families to work on your team, puts in extra time to ensure projects get done, and feels comfortable suggesting new ideas or possible improvements, that's also feedback about you and your VOICE.

People are always telling us how they feel about us, what they think of us, and what they need from us—but not always out loud. We just have to pay attention.

Seek Out Feedback

Provokers don't just recognize feedback when they see it. They also intentionally seek it out—from their bosses, mentors, team members, leadership coaches, customers, and even family and friends. They want to know where they have room to grow, so they ask.

Rich Fairbank encourages leaders at Capital One to seek out feedback from coaches, bosses, and employees. He explained to me:

    ❝I find almost a perfect correlation between the trajectory of people at Capital One and their seeking of feedback, because it's this restless desire to get better. Yet so many people don't take advantage of that because it means being vulnerable, and people feel uncomfortable being vulnerable. But when a person is vulnerable and says, "These are the things that I need to work on," people start rooting for that person. If a leader puts himself or herself up on a pedestal and tries to act like they don't have issues, then it's human nature to tear the person down.

The minute people think you're not as good as you think you are, they move into the mode of discounting everything about you. But if you're vulnerably trying to get better, and truly want their help, they will help you out.

No matter how successful you get, you always have room to grow. Admitting that and seeking out those opportunities isn't a sign of weakness. It's a sign of greatness.

Use Your Own Judgment

Not all feedback will be useful, and you won't always agree. Consider whether you respect the person's opinion and whether it's the first time you've heard these ideas. If different people keep telling you the same thing, they're probably onto something worth exploring.

Ultimately it's up to you whether to shift your behavior based on the feedback you're getting. If you want to make some changes, you need to become exceptionally aware of when you're falling back into old patterns. The more people you can get to point out when you're doing whatever it is that you want to stop doing, start doing, or doing more or less of, the easier it will be to shift your habits.

At the end of the day, any changes you make should be because you see the benefit of the feedback and want to change, not because someone else thinks you should.

Take It Like a Champ

Asking for feedback is easy, at least compared to receiving it. That's the hard part…and the most rewarding.

I recently decided to try a valuable, eye-opening, and most-ly unpleasant exercise I read about in a book. I asked several friends the same question: What are my top three worst traits? I even gave them a few suggestions for inspiration: Arrogant, hyper, needy, overly opinionated, rigid, nitpicking, passive, indecisive, de-manding, hostile, stuffy, overly sensitive, sly, untrustworthy, abrupt, excessively perky, impulsive, melodramatic, rude, shy, pessimistic, closed-minded.

I knew I was about to hear harsh words; that's exactly what I had asked for. I prepared myself by remembering that I will always have room to grow. Better to know than not know, I thought.

Here was the response of one friend:

Hey M,

I don't especially like doing this, because I think you're wonderful. If you are asking for traits that you could temper, I'd say the below:

Impulsive, Abrupt, and Hyper at times, and not aware of how your behavior impacts others and can make them uncomfortable.

Love you and thanks for trusting me to ask my advice,

M

Ouch! As soon as I read her email, I closed it and pretended not to have read it at all. A couple days later, I opened it again, read it completely, and realized she was right. Now I have a chance to im-prove in these areas, because I'm aware of them. Without awareness it's difficult to change anything.

Some feedback stings, especially when we know it's true. Sometimes it causes such a strong reaction in us that we need some time to let it simmer for a while before responding. The key is to consider all feedback a gift, not a personal attack.

Feedback is really just the opinion of that person. If you respect the individual and see the truth in what he or she is saying, consider the feedback and adjust based on what feels right for you. If you don't agree, just remember: Sticks and stones can break your bones, and words can hurt even more...but only if you let them.

Keep It Coming

When people give you feedback, appreciate them for it. You need their input to continue growing, and no one will keep giving feedback to someone who consistently takes offense or doesn't listen.

As Rich Fairbank puts it, "Everybody is ready to give feedback, but often they hesitate, wondering, 'How violent is this going to be? What are the consequences to me and our relationship?' So be vulnerable, go out there, and soak up the feedback like a sponge. And make people feel safe giving it."

Ask those who give you feedback for specific suggestions that might help you improve. If you choose to take action based on their feedback, do so immediately and let them know what you're doing. We've all met those people who ask for feedback and then do nothing with it. At some point, we stop wasting our breath.

Show the people who are brave and caring enough to be real with you that you truly care what they think, and ask them to keep it coming.

CHAPTER 19

Trust Me

"Trust takes a while to build up, and you can destroy it by being inconsistent with what you say you stand for."

—Ken Blanchard

Even if you know the value of your VOICE, you're going to have a hard time convincing others to listen—that is, until you prove you can be trusted.

To build trust, you must be intentional about your interests. It's good to be on a quest—to reach for something big and to ask for help—but for other people to trust you enough to follow along for the ride, you must be upfront about why you're striving to get opportunities. Otherwise your passion can easily be misinterpreted as selfishness and your vision mislabeled as self-serving.

Who Does She Think She Is?

Several years ago I began considering how to combine my two greatest passions: health and leadership. At different points in my life, I have been a student athlete, personal fitness trainer, and massage therapist. And one of my degrees is in kinesiology—the study of human movement—so providing leadership training to senior-level executives within the health and wellness industry seemed right up my alley.

I began by interviewing leaders in the club industry—highly respected professionals who own and/or operate large-scale gyms. During my initial research, I learned about Norm Cates, a former gym owner, current publisher of Club Insider magazine, and an industry leader for more than 35 years. Norm has a deep passion for the health of our country, which made him someone I wanted to get to know.

So I called him without an appointment. Despite his busy schedule, he talked to me for 45 minutes and then offered to connect me with several other industry leaders. I had meetings scheduled with each of them within the week.

During these interviews, I got so excited to learn their perspectives on general industry issues that I completely lost focus about why I'd wanted to connect with them in the first place— to learn about their leadership challenges. When I received an email from one of the executives I interviewed asking if I was on a "witch hunt," I had no idea what I had done wrong, but something about my approach wasn't working. So I forwarded the note to Norm, whose overwhelmingly candid response felt like a gut-punch. Here's what he had to say:

Misti,

You approached me with the idea of bringing your expertise in leadership training to our industry. But the questions you seek answers for in this and other emails you have copied me on are the same questions all of us have been racking our brains over for decades. For you to divert your research from what you represented to something totally different and much more divergent will get you nowhere fast in the realm of necessary credibility. Take this for what it's intended to be: coaching.

While Norm's response bruised my ego, I knew he was only being cruel to be kind, and his harsh words were meant to redirect, not chastise, me.

My intention had not been to offend or mislead these industry leaders. I simply wanted to understand the greater issues and to help by pointing out challenges, not realizing that I would insult them by assuming they hadn't already identified these issues. Of course they had no interest in my ideas and no reason to care what I thought. They didn't even know me, much less trust me.

Many professionals fall into this trap when they first enter the workforce or start new jobs. They see the problems and want to change things before they've built credibility, which just doesn't work. Suggesting change before understanding the full picture is like running for president without a firm grip on history; it will just make you a laughing stock (as many politicians have proved).

Thanks to some seemingly unkind words from a kind man, I was able to correct course. Rather than offering my two cents on industry issues, I started asking questions, having fun, and building relationships with people I respect.

The sheer idea of provoking requires trust. If trust isn't there, provoking will feel like pushing, like you're manipulating others to do things they don't necessarily want to do. When you're clear about your intentions, and your intentions are greater than to help yourself, people are much more likely to line up behind you in pursuit of the quest.

HIGHLIGHTS
SECTION 3: INTENTIONS

1. Those who provoke greatness are intentional about their decisions and communication—particularly when it comes to vision, values, culture, growth, and employee development.

2. If you're not intentional about your values—both identifying them and living them—you risk losing the trust of your team and your customers, and eventually losing your best people.

3. A shelf full of "best company to work for" trophies might create traction to your company, but if you're not putting your money—and energy—where your mouth is, people won't be fooled for long. Smart leaders intentionally build, not buy, their cultures—making their companies something people decide to brag about.

4. Intentional leaders don't wait until annual reviews to give employees feedback. They communicate clearly and in a timely manner so that people have the information they need to do their very best work. This kind of honesty leads to trust, which opens the door to collaboration and creativity.

5. People can spot the difference between manipulation and motivation. When your intention is to manipulate someone into doing something for your own selfish reasons, you'll fail to provoke greatness.

Section 4: Community

Community: Fostering environments where people feel connected to one another

Companies wanting to attract and retain highly engaged, passionate, dedicated people must fulfill one of our core human drivers, and that's a need for connection.

Understanding this core need is the reason Starbucks, TED (and TEDx), and Crossfit have taken off. Sure, Starbucks sells coffee, TED(x) sells seats, and Crossfit sells fitness. But many other companies sell these same things. So why do these brands have such strong, growing reputations? Because either by accident or on purpose, these companies understand our innate human desire to connect with others. And they have provided customers and employees with environments that allow—and even encourage—this sense of community.

The same desire for connection that attracts customers to these brands also attracts (and retains) passionate, enthusiastic, and driven employees. Now more than ever, people are looking for ways to feel connected to communities that share their beliefs, interests, goals, and passions.

In some neighborhoods around the country, you can get into your car in your garage, pull into the parking deck at work, take an elevator to your office, close the door, and get to work...all without speaking to anyone. You can pump gas, get cash, rent a movie, have dinner, go grocery shopping, and fill prescriptions without ever getting out of your car, and with minimal human contact. We might spend plenty of time communicating with people online, but developing and sustaining meaningful connections usually requires more than emails and Facebook messages.

The increasing lack of opportunities to connect provides a great opportunity for leaders who create purposeful communities—who encourage their teams to create meaningful connections and give them opportunities to do so.

So how do you create this sense of community? By focusing on:

- Vision: Giving them a unifying quest—a vision to work toward and rally around

- Environment: Creating physical environments that give people opportunities to connect

- Events: Planning opportunities to connect around something that isn't work-related

- Vulnerability: Being authentic and transparent, and sharing your ideas and passions

- Achievement: Acknowledging when the team has reached a milestone

- Celebrations: Celebrating successes as well as special dates: anniversaries, birthdays, etc.

- Failure: Failing together, because a team that falls down and pulls each other back up is much stronger because of it

In the following chapters, we'll examine how leaders build communities that provoke greatness in each of these ways.

CHAPTER 20

The Need to Connect

"We cannot live for ourselves alone. Our lives are connected by a thousand invisible threads, and along these sympathetic fibers, our actions run as causes and return to us as results."

—Herman Melville

In previous generations, people fulfilled their need for connection through neighborhood cookouts, church membership, family gatherings, and other community-oriented events.

Today many churchgoers no longer actually go to church. Instead they gather their families around the television or computer to watch videos of their favorite pastors every Sunday. And neighborhood events are quickly becoming a thing of the past. Only 25 percent of people even know their neighbors' names, and 8 percent don't know any of them at all. That's not hard to believe, considering most of us no longer get outdoors and socialize with neighbors. Instead we sit in front of screens.

Yes, we socialize online. Many people have more "friends" on Facebook than in real life. That's the conclusion made by Matthew Brashears, a Cornell University sociologist who found that the number of truly close friends people cite has dropped, even though we're "socializing" as much as ever.

Perhaps this is one reason more people are staying put. Just 11.7 percent of Americans moved to a new home or town in 2013, a huge decline from the 1950s and 1960s—when about 20 percent of people moved every year—and just slightly above the all-time low of 11.6 in 2011.

Economists attribute this to the Great Recession and the still-struggling real-estate market, but considering mobility had already slowed down before the economic crisis began in 2008, I think there's more to it. Moving means leaving family, friends, and neighbors, and starting over in a new community. Staying in one place makes it easier to connect with people and stave off the loneliness.

Something in Common

The need for connection is also why popular sports teams create such an uproar that some companies shut down on days following big games, anticipating employees will have partied too hard to be productive in the office.

I fought this reality when I first moved to Baltimore, Maryland, several years ago. Like many other cities with major sports teams, Baltimore becomes a whole different city when the Ravens play. If you're not up to speed on the game, excited for it, and sporting team colors, you might as well not exist during football season.

If, on the other hand, you show support for the home team, you inevitably wind up in a conversation with someone about the recent game—which can turn into a conversation on more meaningful topics. Many great conversations about passions and interests have begun after first talking a bit of trash about how, "They need to run the ball," or "Now we're not going to make it to the playoffs."

My favorite part? "We're." That's how connected many people feel to their favorite teams, which also happen to be businesses.

Like attracts like. We all want to be a part of communities that clearly believe in the very things we believe in, and which also inspire us. Why do people give years of their lives to the Peace Corps? They certainly don't do it for the money! They do it because they want to feel connected to others who also care about serving the world.

Connections: Your Competitive Advantage

Despite the abundance of LinkedIn connections and Facebook friends, many people are starved for real human interaction—for opportunities to collaborate with likeminded people and have the kind of meaningful conversations that provoke greatness.

Very few companies have figured out how to capitalize on this need.

Creating a sense of community in the workplace is about creating opportunities for people to form bonds and connect over common interests. The more they talk, the more they get to know each other and find their commonalities. The more they learn about their teammates, the more they can trust and be honest with one another, and the more they naturally start to care about one another. And genuinely caring relationships at work lead to better performance and retention. No one wants to leave their friends, especially not when their jobs provide opportunities to grow, plenty of feedback, and the chance to contribute to something greater than themselves.

After decades researching what makes people successful at work, Gallup developed its Q12 Survey—a 12-question assessment that determines whether a company's employees are actively engaged in their work, or just showing up to do the bare minimum and collect a paycheck.

Participants are asked to rate the degree to which each of the following statements are true:

1. I know what is expected of me at work.
2. I have the materials and equipment I need to do my work right.
3. At work, I have the opportunity to do what I do best every day.
4. In the last seven days, I have received recognition or praise for doing good work.
5. My supervisor, or someone at work, seems to care about me as a person.
6. There is someone at work who encourages my development.
7. At work, my opinions seem to count.
8. The mission or purpose of my organization makes me feel

my job is important.

9. My associates or fellow employees are committed to doing quality work.

10. I have a best friend at work.

11. In the last six months, someone at work has talked to me about my progress.

12. This last year, I have had opportunities at work to learn and grow.

Notice that "I got a raise" and "I make lots of money" didn't make the list. Instead more than half of these statements relate directly to having a sense of community and camaraderie at work.

So what does this mean for the bottom line? Companies scoring in the top half on Gallup's Q12 employee-engagement survey are nearly twice as successful as those in the bottom half. Friendship at work is particularly important for employee engagement. People who report having a best friend at work are:

- 43 percent more likely to report having received praise or recognition for their work in the last seven days

- 37 percent more likely to report that someone at work encourages their development

- 35 percent more likely to report coworker commitment to quality

- 28 percent more likely to report that in the last six months, someone at work has talked to them about their progress

- 27 percent more likely to report that the mission of their company makes them feel their job is important

- 27 percent more likely to report that their opinions seem to count at work

- 21 percent more likely to report that at work, they have the opportunity to do what they do best every day

And that's just people who have one strong connection at work!

Imagine the difference it makes when entire teams feel connected to each other and to the success of the organization. Don't get me wrong. Companies without a strong sense of community will still find people to do the work, especially if it's mindless, repetitive work. But for jobs that require thinking, understanding the customer, collaborating, and innovating, you need a cohesive team of people who actually like and support each other as they work to achieve the vision.

CHAPTER 21

Bumping into Each Other: Creating Environments that Connect Your Team

"The kinds of errors that cause plane crashes are invariably errors of teamwork and communication."

—Malcolm Gladwell, from *Outliers*

While most of us want to talk to and connect with others, we don't always make it a priority. It's sort of like healthy eating. We know an apple a day will keep the doctor away, but a chocolate bar is so much tastier!

It's easier to spend time alone or with our closest friends and family than it is to deal with strangers. When we spend time with people we don't know very well, we have to be careful about what we say and do. We're not yet comfortable being ourselves, because we don't know how they will react. But the more time we spend with people, the more comfortable we get with them, until those new faces become familiar.

People work better with those they know, like, and trust. But these types of relationships are hard to build when you hardly ever speak to your colleagues. That's why many leaders have gotten intentional about the design of their workspaces.

Fancy Seeing You Here

When Steve Jobs built a large atrium in the middle of the Pixar Studios headquarters, many considered it a waste of space, but he had a good reason. He had a vision for creating community between departments that almost never interacted with each other, and the open space ensured people would constantly talk to each other, build relationships, and innovate together.

This is the same reason Google has cafeteria-style lunch rooms, game rooms, lounge areas, and the like. It's the reason employees at SPARC (including senior leaders) don't have assigned desks—so that employees have the opportunity to sit next to different people each day. And it's the reason Tony Hsieh spent $350 million of his own money to create an inconvenient office space for his team.

Why Tony Hsieh Is Inconveniencing His Team

While many leaders have given thought to community-centered workspaces, Tony Hsieh, CEO of Zappos, has taken the concept to a whole new level.

The relatively new Zappos building, located in downtown Las Vegas, isn't your typical office space. With only one exit and one central restroom, employees have no choice but to bump into each other—giving them ample opportunities to talk, get to know each other, dream up new ideas, and figure out new ways to collaborate.

As Zach Ware, head developer of the new Zappos campus, explains:

> 66 Our goal is not to create an office space that you take photos of and you say "Wow, that's beautiful." We're incredibly function-oriented. Zappos' core focus is on company culture and the relationships between employees. To enhance that, as odd as it sounds, parts of the office are deliberately inconvenient. The idea is, by [giving employees one way to enter and exit the building] we create a collision point where people are more likely to connect to each other, rather than having them be isolated and never see each other.

While Hsieh's Las Vegas building might not win any architecture awards, Zappos has certainly won the hearts of its employees…and customers.

This is why Zappos no longer needs to seek out highly motivated, talented, driven, respectful employees. The company now receives upwards of 100 résumés a day. Zappos even offers $100 to any prospective employee who does not accept a job offer, and $1,000 to any employee who quits. This is a great way to protect the community—the connection inherent among Zappos employees, customers, and fans.

Tony Hsiesh did more than build a great company with excellent products and services; he built a community, one that's connected by a common vision. And he did so intentionally.

Want to Do What Zappos Did?

Tony Hsieh has clearly laid out the formula for success. So if you want your team to perform at the level of excellence that his does, all you have to do is close off the extra entrances and exits to your building, and your team will start collaborating, right?

Nope. There simply isn't an exact prescription for success. Not with leadership, and certainly not with community building. There is, however, a prescription for discovering what will work best for your company.

It's never just the open floor plan, the centralized entrance/exit, or the communal restrooms. These things can encourage connection, sharing, collaboration, innovation, and the like, but at the end of the day, if your intention is simply to get people to produce more, it's unlikely to work. If, on the other hand, your intention is to create a collaborative environment—where the company, employees, and customers succeed—you will uncover the best possible setup to achieve that result.

Author David Zweig points out several failed attempts to create connections through shared spaces. He writes:

Consider the experience of Scandinavian Airlines (SAS). In 1987 the company redesigned its headquarters around a central "street" that linked a café, shopping, and medical, sports, and other facilities, including several "multirooms" containing comfortable furniture, coffeemakers, fax and photocopying machines, and office supplies. The new design was explicitly intended to promote informal interactions, and management broadcast the message that employees should find opportunities in the new space for "impromptu meetings" and "creative encounters."

What happened as a result? Very little. A study of employee interactions revealed that just 9% were occurring in the street and the café, and just 27% in all the other public spaces combined. In spite of the thoughtfulness and good intentions informing the new design, two-thirds of interactions were still confined to private offices. What went wrong?

Common sense, it turns out, is a poor guide when it comes to designing for interaction. Take the growing enthusiasm for replacing private offices with open floor plans in order to encourage community and collaboration. More than a dozen studies have examined the behavioral effects of such redesigns. There's some evidence that removing physical barriers and bringing people closer to one another does promote casual interactions. But there's a roughly equal amount of evidence that because open spaces reduce privacy, they don't foster informal exchanges and may actually inhibit them. Some studies show that employees in open-plan spaces, knowing that they may be overheard or interrupted, have shorter and more superficial discussions than they otherwise would.

In other words, what works for one company won't necessarily work for the next. Just as every relationship is different—and what makes one relationship successful can wreck another—every company and every team is different. You have to let your own VOICE, and those of your team members, guide your efforts to create connections.

Leaders at Charleston-based tech company SPARC have done a great job of designing their office space to promote community and strengthen their unique company culture. Inspired by Tony Hsieh's redesign, John Smith, the guy who was in charge of SPARC's culture at that time, visited the Las Vegas headquarters, got a feel for what Zappos was doing, and then put his own spin on it.

Having heard about SPARC through my research on excellence in company culture, I drove nine hours just to see what they were up to. While I could certainly see the Zappos influence—limited entrances and centralized bathrooms—SPARC had its own unique community going on.

After my tour, I got to watch the teams in action. SPARC employees don't have assigned desks, only lockers to store their stuff, and it's fascinating to see how they work out the use of space. One team comes together, pulls out their laptops, and talks about whatever project they're working on. When they finish their discussion, some stay where they are to work, while the rest disperse to other groups for other meetings.

The engineering team is a whole different bunch of people. Secluded in the conference room with the lights out and their headsets on, they are clearly a focused group who appreciate solitude. And that's OK too.

As I watched the team at work, it struck me that each team seemed to have its own mini-culture, but still willingly worked with other teams. And, of course, the company as a whole has its own culture. John and the other senior leaders at SPARC found a way to build a space that supports everyone.

SPARC also provides the staff with beer and food on Friday afternoons, to promote a little team bonding after hours. Because after all, the team that plays together, stays together.

Long-Distance Communities

Today 3.1 million U.S. employees work from home full time. That's 2.5 percent of the workforce, excluding self-employed individuals. Creating opportunities for people to come together and form community isn't easy for any leader, but it's even harder when employees don't share an office. So how do you promote community if members of your virtual team rarely or never see each other?

1. Make time for small talk: Virtual teams don't get the chance to bump into one another, socialize, and just catch up. So take the time before every meeting to do both a personal and professional check-in with each person. Encourage employees to share not only what they're working on, but also what's going on in their lives.

2. Provide the right tools: There are many excellent Cloud-based platforms that let teams share files, access secure information from anywhere, and determine who's working and who's away from the "office." Your team also needs communication tools like instant messenger and video conferencing. This cuts down on the need for crazy-long email threads and lets team members have face-to-face conversations, make eye contact, and share a smile or laugh—all important methods of bonding.

3. Get the gang together. Bring the whole group (or as many as you can) together as often as possible. If your team is too spread out for this to be a reality, consider getting small groups together based on the region where they're located.

4. Invest in online resources that let team members learn about each other: Build an internal social network for employees to share information about their ongoing projects, areas of interest, professional experience, and personal passions. Or simply create a private Facebook page. Just be sure to use it and encourage your team to do so.

5. Help like minds find each other: The more you know about individuals on your team, the more opportunities you have to create connections between those with shared interests.

For more ways to create connections between virtual teams, visit www.MeasurableGreatness.com/HowToProvoke.

CHAPTER 22

After Hours: Connecting Your Team When They're Off the Clock

"Communication leads to community, that is, to understanding, intimacy, and mutual valuing."

—Rollo May

Fostering connections inside the workplace is a great way to build community. But the most meaningful connections are often formed outside the office, when people are more likely to let their guards down and talk about themselves, rather than just the work at hand.

This is why leaders who are serious about creating community give their teams opportunities to connect after hours, so they get to know and trust each other, and begin to enjoy one another's company.

River Rocks

Shared experiences, good or bad, are one of the quickest ways to form connections. When we go through something together, or have experienced something that other people haven't, it gives us common ground, an unspoken understanding, and something to talk about.

I witnessed this phenomenon in action last Thanksgiving, when my friend Sally and I decided to cook dinner for two retired, down-on-their-luck Vietnam vets: Don, who lives in her storage facility, and Charles, who did some renovations on my new home.

We set a date, invited them over, and began preparing our menu. I was so excited about having the opportunity to connect with and give back to these two heroes. And I couldn't wait to hear their stories.

Just before Charles arrived, Don handed me a rock and said, "It's one of my nicest diamonds." Without hesitation, I examined it, told him it was beautiful, and asked where he found it. I didn't care that it wasn't a real diamond. I was just glad he got to feel good about giving me a gift.

Charles and Don bonded over dinner while sharing their war stories. They talked about their experiences at the Ho Chi Minh trail and how dangerous it was. Don said that once his boots were on the ground, his life expectancy was 16 seconds. Sixteen seconds! These men were walking miracles, no doubt.

Just before dessert, Charles asked Don what he does for a living. "I sell gold and diamonds," Don said. Don then reached into his pocket and pulled out something wrapped in aluminum foil. As he opened the foil, Charles waited in anticipation to see what was inside.

When Don pulled out the "diamonds," we all oohed and aahed at his precious gems—except for Charles, who took one look and said, "Dude, those are river rocks!"

I held my breath, waiting for Don's reaction and wishing Charles had played along so Don wouldn't feel like a crazy person. But Don never disagreed with Charles. He simply admired his diamonds for a few more seconds and then passed them around the table.

Later that night, as I reflected on the evening, I kept thinking about how effortless it was for Charles to speak the truth. I wondered why Don didn't disagree with Charles and insist the rocks were diamonds. It was as if they had an unspoken agreement to be real. Both of them had shared several hard stories about the impact the war had on their lives. Those shared experiences connected them.

Several weeks later, while chatting with Charles, I discovered that my hunch was true. "That Don is a bit nutty," he remarked. "But who wouldn't be after what we've been through?"

Different Venue, Different Vibe

This is what happens when people share common interests, challenges, and passions—whether it's past experience, a hobby, the fact they made it through a merger together, that they're both parents, or even just that they like the same bands or TV shows. I have several friends who watch certain shows live every week because their coworkers also watch them, and the whole team looks forward to discussing new episodes the following morning at the office.

Common interests, even if it's nothing more than a fictional story, give people a reason to share, fostering connection and trust—important ingredients to highly collaborative, innovative teams. It is through our commonalities that connections are created and community is built. So the more chances we have to share time with people, without an agenda, the greater our chances are for building trust. But when we are just focused on work, we don't always make time for bonding or allow ourselves to be vulnerable enough to have the getting-to-know you conversations.

This is why team-building activities have become all the rage. Google registers more than a million hits when you run a search for "team building." Some companies spend millions of dollars each year on ropes courses, group trips, company outings to support local charities, sports events, and corporate retreats. These group activities give team members a chance to strengthen bonds, which ultimately lead to better working relationships, better team outcomes, and a better bottom line.

When Zenimax Online Studios, a video game company located in Hunt Valley, Maryland, takes the entire company to the movies, they create opportunities for team members to share experiences. Rather than simply asking about a pending project, they wind up talking about the movie before getting down to business. As a result, employees have a greater sense of connection and care for one another.

Teams who have gone through ropes courses together often wind up with excellent content for meaningful discussions. Just imagine what would happen if your boss was in a position on a ropes course that literally scared him, and you got to help him make it through that part of the course.

There's simply an unspoken trust that emerges when we go

through challenges together. We get the chance to be a little bit vulnerable with each other—and to feel that it's OK to do so, just as Don and Charles knew it was OK to expose their true selves with each other.

Create Opportunities, but Don't Force It

Although creating opportunities for your team to connect is part of your opportunity as a leader, it's important to remember that one size does not fit all when it comes to team-building exercises. Some groups might go through a ropes course and come out closer than ever, while another group might genuinely despise outdoorsy activities. Or if there's already a lot of drama on your team, they might resent being forced to spend a day in the heat pretending to trust each other.

The key is considering what your team would actually enjoy doing together, not forcing them to do things they don't want to do or spend time with people they don't enjoy or care to get to know. If you don't know what they want to do, just ask. Then make arrangements and let them take the lead.

My friend Cory, who recently left a company he'd been with for years, shared with me the perfect example of what not to do. Cory worked for his former employer from the time it was a small startup run by a flip-flop-wearing entrepreneur until after the company went public and brought on a new leadership team.

The company had an annual sales meeting every January at a remote location with warmer weather and beaches. For four days, the entire sales team and leaders from across the company would do a quick review of the previous year, highlighting past accomplishments and challenges, and then plan a strategy for the new year.

"It was an opportunity for the team—most of whom worked remotely—to have a few days together," Cory recalls. "Yes, we were sitting in meetings all day, but then we'd have dinners, happy hours, and casual events. Naturally there was a lot of camaraderie and just catching up with friends, peers, and co-workers in a somewhat relaxed setting. We all looked forward to it."

Years later, after the company had grown and taken on a new executive team, the sales director took the team to Puerto Rico. Cory and his fellow sales reps were thrilled. Who wouldn't want to go to Puerto Rico in January? Problem was, the new exec changed the structure of the retreat, most of which was spent learning a new sales training methodology.

"Don't get me wrong," Cory said. "Training has its place, but it was forced on everyone." In order to fit it into this one week, the team was in meetings and break-out groups from early morning until 11:00 or 12:00 at night, working non-stop indoors with no windows. "The hotel was literally on the beach, but we had no time to go outside, get some fresh air, and decompress with friends we hadn't seen much in the past year."

On the last day, the team finally got an afternoon off to spend time together, but with one caveat. Rather than choosing who to socialize with, everyone was assigned to a group of people with whom they didn't normally work.

"Our only free time was spent with people we didn't know," Cory said. "We had these forced team-building exercises on the beach, but it was just awkward because we were competing with people we'd never met or talked to before. If we had done these exercises with our actual teams, the people we wanted to be with, they might have helped morale. Instead everyone despised it. Instead of getting pumped for the new year, we were annoyed that we had to leave our families for a week, when we could have just done the training at a hotel in town."

Cory's bad team-building experience is not uncommon. In fact, most people prefer unstructured bonding opportunities. And while 66 percent of workers have been made to participate in some form of team-building activity, 54 percent say doing more of these activities would not help them work better with colleagues.

Bottom line: Connections are stronger when they happen naturally. So give your team chances to spend time together outside of work, then let them take the lead.

CHAPTER 23

4 Fears that Can Cripple Your Community

"The absence of love, belonging, and connection always leads to suffering."
—Brené Brown, from *Daring Greatly*

Most leaders want the benefits of a strong work community. They even go so far as to schedule team-building exercises, plan ice-breaker games for team meetings, and make it a point to learn about their employees. Problem is, sometimes they unintentionally undermine the communities they're working to build—usually because they're leading from fear rather than vision and vulnerability.

Here are four ways fear can manifest itself and cripple the community you've worked so hard to build:

- Fear of the unknown
- Fear of never advancing
- Fear of authenticity
- Fear of breaking the rules

Fear of the Unknown

The kind of communities that promote innovation and collaboration are born out of passion and vision. Fear breeds mistrust, hoarding, and responsibility dodging—all of which can tear a community apart from the inside out.

Fear of competition is especially problematic in companies or industries where there's a lack of upward mobility or the future is particularly uncertain. For example, I recently gave a speech to a group of leaders from a local university. In preparation for my presentation, I dove into research on higher education. I also surveyed my audience about their greatest fears and concerns.

The research is clear: Education is going through a major transformation, and most colleges have not yet adjusted for the new world of learning. So it wasn't surprising that my audience survey revealed the educators' greatest challenge is "fear of competition." Not wanting to lose their jobs, competition has fueled the culture at this particular university (and probably many others).

The day after my speech, I shared what I'd learned with the president of the university. "Your staff members are afraid for their jobs," I told him, thinking this might alarm him.

"Good," he said. "I want them to be afraid. Fear necessitates action."

"Fear is one way to motivate, I suppose."

"It's the only way," he demanded. "They won't get into action if they don't see a strong reason for it."

His perspective is not unique. In fact, this line of thinking explains why most marketing is aimed at motivating away from loss, rather than toward gain. This is what I call a scarcity mindset, and it might work in sales, but it does not provoke greatness; it provokes fear and unproductive competition. When employees are scared about what they might lose—their jobs, their resources, their opportunities—they waste time worrying when they could be focused on their work. They hoard resources and information when they could be collaborating.

Rather than lead through scarcity of resources—such as money, materials, talent, and clients—focus on the greater outcomes you've promised both your customers and employees. This type of thinking sets you up to create a company culture where people naturally work toward achieving the vision.

Like many industries, education is changing rapidly, and innovation is critical. But is innovation possible in the face of such self-doubt, lack of collaboration, and fear of failure? How can people think big, much less share ideas, when they're wasting energy fearing for their jobs?

Imagine how much better this team could function if the educators trusted one another enough to pull together, get creative, and get into action together, rather than competing with each other and hoarding information. My guess is they'd be much more likely to find ways the university could not only succeed in an ever-changing environment, but excel and set new standards for higher learning. They'd have stronger buy-in, brilliant ideas, and more value to offer students.

Those with a scarcity mindset are afraid of giving up their rigid beliefs, so they drive good people away by creating cultures that foster an "every man for himself" mentality. On the other hand, leaders who operate from an abundance mindset—believing there's plenty to go around—end up with positive, welcoming cultures where people collaborate and support one another as they work to achieve the vision.

So what's necessary to create this shift away from fear and toward innovation? Brené Brown says it best: "Vulnerability is the birthplace of innovation, creativity, and change."

Leaders who want to create collaborative, innovative environments must stop using fear to motivate. Instead they must open up the table for honest discussions, reveal their own fears, envision an even better future, and share it consistently.

Otherwise fear will infect the community, opening the door for mistrust, bickering, and resentment.

Fear of Never Advancing

Having a clear lack of opportunities to advance also causes unhealthy competition in a workplace. When employees view career advancement opportunities as scarce, they're more likely to stop sharing resources and helping each other. They destroy meaningful connections with colleagues, and it becomes an all-about-me game, rather than a team-focused environment.

I recently interviewed a seasoned sales pro who left a job he'd had for years. The No. 1 reason he originally took the job was upward mobility, and it was also the No. 1 reason he ultimately left the company. The ability to develop professional skills and career trajectory is critical, at least for those who care about their results, thus their careers. Not everyone is interested in rising up the ranks, and many employees will tolerate mediocrity in themselves and their employers. Yet most employers say they want high-achievers.

Provoking greatness in others means refusing to settle for mediocrity, and instead commanding excellence. It means creating opportunities for people to advance, and corporate cultures where people trust that their leaders are invested in helping them grow and advance. Otherwise high-achievers will find other opportunities where they can really shine.

In fact, a lack of upward mobility is one of the main reasons people quit their jobs. CareerBuilder surveyed 3,008 people at the end of 2013, asking who planned to change jobs in 2014 and why. Half of all respondents said they would look for new work. When asked why, four of the top seven answers were related to career advancement, including:

- 65 percent didn't feel valued by their employers.
- 45 percent were dissatisfied with advancement opportunities at their current companies.
- 39 percent felt underemployed.
- 36 percent felt they had been overlooked for a promotion.

Create a culture where excellence is recognized and rewarded—where no one has reached his or her limits—and you'll provoke greatness as they rise to the occasion.

Fear of Authenticity

When you pretend to know more than you do—for the sake of being seen as competent—you miss out on the opportunities inherent in sharing challenges. When you are willing to be vulnerable—to share your lack of knowledge or understanding—you set the tone for authenticity and open the door for meaningful connections.

Robert, an engineer who works for a government contracting firm, experienced this firsthand. "Trust has been an issue since I came on board," he told me. "People don't want to share information and work together because they're not sure if keeping the information to themselves is safer, which makes collaboration and getting stuff done an issue."

Thankfully a new president—one who is authentic and transparent—was hired and has managed to prove she is trustworthy.

"There was a great deal of tension about what was going to happen to our pensions and health insurance," Robert explained. "People were rightfully concerned and spending time at the office thinking and talking about their fears, rather than focusing on the work."

So the president brought the entire team—several hundred employees—together and shared the raw numbers, making it clear that unless something changed, the company would be out of business within five to 10 years. "When she explained the situation and what needed to be done as a result, it all made perfect sense," Robert said. "Everyone rallied to help the company overcome the challenges we were facing."

This kind of transparency is the door to trust. If you want people to trust you, you have to trust them. Pretending you know everything and have never made a mistake will weaken your team quickly. If you're willing to lie about your abilities or challenges, what else are you going to lie about? On the other hand, if you're open and honest, you create a trusting, open environment that fosters deeper, more trusting connections.

Fear of Breaking the Rules

Rules often save lives. Roads have speed limits to minimize danger in the case of car accidents. Most states have outlawed texting while driving for the same reason. And hospitals no longer allow anyone to smoke on the premises (even outside), given the health concerns of their clientele.

Every business, organization, and even family has rules in place to keep people safe. But sometimes rules cause more harm than good—especially when employees are more focused on avoiding trouble than serving the community (both internal and external).

Case in point: When my friend and former neighbor, Mayra, called me twice before 10 a.m., I knew something must be wrong. With a shaky and fearful voice, she explained, "I just fell again. I need help. How far are you from the building?"

"Twenty minutes," I said. "I'm jumping in the car now!"

"No, no," she said. "My husband will beat you here. I was hoping you were in the building."

I had just moved out of the apartment building where Mayra still lives. Being paralyzed from the waist down, she had lost her balance in the bathroom and could not get herself back upright. Trying not to hit her head against the tile wall in her shower, she managed to pull her cell phone from her pocket and dial for help.

"Do you know anyone in the building who can help?" she asked. "I'm not sure how long I can hold on."

Feeling helpless, I hung up and called the building's management office. "This is an emergency," I told the guy who answered the phone. "Mayra is falling in her apartment and needs help right away."

"You need to call the police," he said.

He clearly didn't understand the urgency of the situation, which infuriated me. Mayra had lived in the building for two years, and all the employees knew about her condition. "She will fall if someone doesn't go help her…right now," I demanded.

"We're not allowed to enter any apartment without the police."

I hung up and called my old neighbor Pete, who rushed to Mayra's apartment, got her upright, and asked how else he could help.

Thank goodness for Pete, but I'm still baffled by the staff's unwillingness to help. I know there are rules in place to protect residents' privacy, but in a potentially life-threatening situation, those rules aren't helping anyone. The same is true in any workplace—even when no one's life is on the line. Rules are meant to be broken, especially when they limit our humanity.

This is why Tony Hsieh gives employees the freedom to do whatever they think is necessary to care for customers. For example, a woman whose husband died in a car accident called to ask about returning boots she'd purchased for him before his death. Not only did the call-center rep help with the return, she also ordered flowers for the widow, without asking a supervisor, and billed them to the company.

As Hsieh explains, "At the funeral, the widow told her friends and family about the experience. Not only was she a customer for life, but so were those 30 or 40 people at the funeral."

No wonder Zappos is one of the fastest-growing Internet retailers of all time. That's what happens when you put people before rules. That's what happens when leaders put community and connection at the center of their business plan.

So how do you ensure that your rules aren't leaving the members of your community feeling disempowered and disconnected? You give members of the community a voice in the rules that govern them.

A friend of mine once suggested that the government moves so slowly because there are so many unnecessary, outdated rules. At the time they were created, the rules were necessary, but then the world changed, and the rules did not go away. His idea was to put a timeline for review on every rule. So every 10 years, a rule would disappear unless the legislators clearly decide it's critical to keep. While I don't know if that strategy would work for government, the idea behind it could be a powerful tool for companies, but perhaps with a shorter timeframe for review.

Taking a play from Hsieh's playbook, it's good practice to set as few hard-and-fast rules as possible, trusting that you've hired competent people who will make good decisions without being told what to do. Then for the rules that are deemed necessary, be sure to review them on a predetermined timeframe to ensure they're still helping—and not hurting—the members of your community.

Just imagine what a difference it could have made for one of the employees at the apartment building to get to Mayra just in the nick of time. Those are the types of opportunities that leave people feeling connected to what they do and who they serve.

HIGHLIGHTS
SECTION 4: COMMUNITY

1. We all want to be a part of communities that clearly believe in the very things we believe in, and which also inspire us.

2. People are starved for human connection. Companies that provide a sense of community attract people who collaborate and innovate together as they work toward the vision.

3. People work better with those they know, like, and trust. That's why many leaders are building workspaces that encourage team members to mingle and collaborate.

4. Meaningful connections are often formed outside the office, when people are more likely to let their guards down and talk about themselves, rather than just the work at hand.

5. Fear breeds mistrust, hoarding, and dodging responsibility—all of which can tear a community apart from the inside out.

Section 5: Energy

Energy: Having passion and unstoppable drive at the highest level within a company

Have you ever sat through a meeting, sucking down coffee and pretending to listen— then walked out and headed straight to Starbucks? Evidently your regular office coffee isn't strong enough!

Have you ever stood in line, waiting for your turn, only to get caught up in a conversation with someone who clearly needs a therapist—after which you were completely exhausted, so you grabbed a chocolate bar for an energy boost?

Have you ever felt comatose after enjoying a tasty meal, even though you hoped that three-inch-thick, triple-chocolate desert would give you just the extra bit of energy you needed to finish the project awaiting you at the office?

I've never had any of those experiences because I always walk out on any meeting that bores me, flat-out ignore the person in line, and eat nothing but protein and veggies. HA!

The truth: I admire people who are that good at protecting their energy, because it's a valuable resource, especially for those who want to provoke greatness. Energy is contagious, so whatever vibes you're putting out there, your team is picking up—for better or for worse.

The essence of energy is having the amount you need to do the things that are important to you. It's about filling your days with tasks and people who boost your energy, rather than use it up or leave you feeling drained. It's about finishing each day with that feeling of deep satisfaction that your time and energy went into something meaningful to you.

As a leader, it's also about helping your team feel the same way.

Energy is the foundation of provoking greatness in yourself and others. In fact, the right or wrong kind of energy (or a lack of energy) can make or break your ability to do so.

You want commitment of passion, persistence, and unstoppable drive at the highest level from your team? You want employees who have passion for the work they've committed to and who will take ownership of their results? You want employees who are connected to each other and feel like part of a community?

Most leaders do! Yet few understand that passionate, dedicated people, who take full ownership of their results, are attracted to—and thrive in—positive, happy environments. Passion, at its core, is directed energy. Persistence and unstoppable drive—the kind that keep people moving toward achieving the vision (or quest)—require energy. And for employees to feel positive connections with one another, there must be...(you guessed it)...positive energy.

When you do a good job with the first four elements of VOICE (vision, ownership, intentions, and community), you set a tone for the right kind of productive, positively directed energy. But maintaining that momentum means you have to keep your energy going strong.

So how do you protect and add to the energy of everyone around you?

1. Understand that energy is contagious and be conscious of the energy you project.

2. Take care of yourself and protect your own energy levels.

3. Know what activities, subjects, and people add to your energy levels—and which take away from it.

4. Protect the energy of your team by hiring people who bring the right kind of energy to work.

In this section, we'll discuss why energy matters and what it takes to create and maintain the right kind of energy for your team.

CHAPTER 24

Happy Workplace, Healthy Bottom Line

"Happy CEOs are more likely to lead teams of employees who are both happy and healthy, and who find their work climate deuces to high-performance. What this means is that companies and leaders who take measures to cultivate a happy workplace will not only have more productive and efficient workers—they'll have less absenteeism and lower healthcare expenditures."

—Shawn Achor, from *The Happiness Advantage*

Cultivating happiness in your work is an ongoing process where you continue to grow, learn, achieve, set goals, have new experiences, and connect with others around meaningful work. That last one is particularly important, considering the fact most adults spend more waking hours at work than at home.

Yet most people aren't happy with their jobs. Shawn Achor, author of *The Happiness Advantage*, summarizes the state of happiness in U.S. workplaces:

> A Conference Board survey released in January 2010 found that only 45% of workers surveyed were happy at their jobs, the lowest in 22 years of polling. Depression rates today are 10 times higher than they were in 1960. Every year that age threshold of unhappiness sinks lower, not just at universities but across the nation. 50 years ago, the mean onset age of depression was 29.5 years old. Today, it is almost exactly half that: 14.5 years old.

...As a society, we know very well how to be unwell and miserable and so little about how to thrive.

Since then the Conference Board's job satisfaction numbers have risen to 47.7 percent, but the majority of Americans still aren't happy at work.

Who Cares if They're Happy?

Why does happiness at work matter? And why should leaders make it a focus and priority? Said simply, happy employees bring more to the team. Happy workers are 50 percent more motivated than their unhappy colleagues, and 180 percent more energized. They also spend 80 percent of their workweek actually doing their jobs, while unhappy workers spend only 40 percent of their time at the office focused on what they're being paid to do. That's two days per week of actual work.

Focus isn't all happy employees bring to the table. Jessica Pryce-Jones, author of Happiness at Work: Maximizing Your Psychological Capital for Success, outlines a few more key advantages of happy workforces. She writes:

> **" "** Our empirical research, involving 9,000 people from around the world, reveals some astonishing findings. Employees who report being happiest at work:
> - Stay twice as long in their jobs as their least happy colleagues
> - Spend double their time at work focused on what they are paid to do
> - Take ten times less sick leave
> - Believe they are achieving their potential twice as much

Happiness at work matters—not just because happy people are more pleasant to be around, but because happier people work harder, contribute more, build community, and pass their positive energy on to everyone around them.

Happiness Is Contagious

Energy is catching. We all know people who are never happy, who complain all the time and feel sorry for themselves. And most of us avoid these people like the plague, not wanting to be infected with their negativity. On the other hand, we flock to happy, upbeat people, because we absolutely want to catch what they have.

Happiness is a particularly powerful contagion—creating a ripple effect that impacts the mindset of everyone you know, and even the people they know. When researchers from Harvard Medical School and the University of California, San Diego, studied the happiness of nearly 5,000 individuals over a period of 20 years, they found that when an individual becomes happy, the network effect can be measured up to three degrees—meaning a person's happiness triggers a chain reaction that benefits not only her friends, but her friends' friends, and her friends' friends' friends. And the effect isn't fleeting. It can last up to a year.

For leaders who want to provoke greatness, bringing the right kind of energy to work is crucial, because happiness—or lack thereof—spreads exponentially when it starts at the top. If your team is moping around or walking on eggshells, you've probably been spreading some negative energy, and they've gotten infected. If they are energetic and enthusiastic about their work, you're probably doing something right.

My friend Dora is an executive in the entertainment industry. Her office has its own kitchen—fully equipped with enough staff to feed roughly 200 staffers during a 90-minute period each afternoon at lunch. One day Dora happened to be walking through the kitchen at the end of the lunch cycle and overheard the head cook yell out, "Awesome job, everyone! We're getting tighter and tighter. Good work today!"

Inspired by what she witnessed, Dora went back to her desk and wrote a personal email to the head cook, telling her, "You're a good leader for our kitchen. I loved the way you cheered your team on. It's inspiring. Keep up the good work!"The very next day, when Dora walked into the kitchen, the head cook rushed over, gave her a hug, and thanked her for the email.

"Thank you," Dora responded. The cook's positive energy did more than just inspire the hardworking kitchen staff. It inspired everyone who witnessed the cook's energetic leadership in action, including Dora.

"Her cheerleading put a smile on my face," Dora told me. "She unknowingly prompted me to look for opportunities to do the same with my own team."

So what kind of vibes are you putting out? How do you know? Just look at your team. Do they spend the majority of their time complaining and watching the clock? Or do they actually seem happy to be there—to be part of your team and part of achieving your vision?

Whatever the answer, it says just as much about your energy as it does about theirs. Happiness at work matters—not just to your bottom line, but to the success of every person on your team.

Don't Worry, Be Happy

In Geography of Bliss, Eric Weiner chronicles his journey to understand happiness—what causes it and what keeps it at bay. A simple question, but not an easy one to answer. So he did more than hit the books. He traveled the world, meeting with leading happiness researchers and poring over their data. He also visited the happiest and unhappiest counties in the world, interviewing people in each region about their lives.

Here's what I took away about increasing happiness:

1. Be relational. Put time and energy into building relationships, connecting people, sharing about yourself, helping others, and giving back. As Wein-

er writes: "Social scientists estimate that about 70 percent of our happiness stems from our relationships, both quantity and quality, with friends, family, coworkers, and neighbors."

2. Smile more. The impact of your body language—particularly your facial expression—is huge. What does yours say most of the time?

3. Appreciate people who make a difference for you. Once you go looking for reasons to say "thank you," you'll find them everywhere.

4. Live as close to nature as possible and spend plenty of time outside.

5. Trust. If you don't trust people, don't hire them.

6. Practice patience. Many impatient leaders want new hires to have it all figured out already, but that can take time.

7. Let go of your expectations. Expectations are dangerous. Decide to reach excellence, work at it, and then appreciate the results.

8. Suppress envy, either by hiding what you have or sharing it. In the case of workplaces, I suggest sharing as much as possible.

9. Compete with a collaborative mindset. Most people are competitive; they want to win. But working together to achieve a greater outcome is at the heart of collaboration, connection, and happiness.

10. Make failure a goal. Great leaders put important work in the hands of those they know will stretch and grow, which means inevitably failing at times.

Weiner writes, "The crap allows the good stuff to grow." (Failure is fertilizer. Love that!)

11. Be naïve. Having a beginner's mindset is valuable in all areas of life, including leadership. Approach all tasks with a sense of naivety, and you'll always learn from the experience.

12. Take ownership. If something bothers you, do something about it. Rather than complain, keep asking, "How can I get a better result?"

13. Count your acts of kindness…every single week. Why? Because you always get what you focus on. The more you focus on kind acts, the more kind acts will surface.

For more on increasing your happiness—and that of your team—visit www.MeasurableGreatness.com/HowToProvoke.

CHAPTER 25

Is Your Passion Productive?

"When you go from feeling energized, excited, and in control of your work to feeling an overwhelming compulsion to achieve and produce, you've tipped from helpful harmonious passion into harmful obsessive passion."
—Elizabeth Grace Saunders

Like happiness, passion can be a great source of energy and an effective vehicle for boosting the energy levels of everyone around you. But passion isn't always a good thing. Think of it like electricity: When it's harnessed—i.e., focused around a meaningful vision—it generates enough energy to power your vision. But when it isn't grounded, it can blow people away.

This is an important distinction for leaders, because the same passion that can draw people to you can also send them running in the other direction. Just consider the following two examples.

Too Hot to Handle

I met with Doug, a CEO in the financial industry, to discuss my executive coaching services. He was considering bringing me on board and wanted to ensure my coaching style matched his belief system. Knowing I was meeting with a brilliant, successful businessman, I expected the interview to be rigorous, but his intensity caught me off guard.

I started our meeting by asking Doug a few questions about his background and leadership style. Disregarding my attempts to begin building a relationship, he ignored my questions and immediately redirected the conversation to what I could do for his company.

His concentrated stare was off-putting, and I quickly understood why the executive who arranged our meeting seemed afraid of him. So I jumped right into my methodology and style. I felt like I was in a bullpen with someone who might charge at any moment. His intensity was exhausting!

After 10 minutes that felt like hours, I sat back in my chair, maintained eye contact, and asked, "Do you get how intense you are?"

Doug explained that his company conducted a 360-assessment of him several years ago, from which he learned that his team was terrified of him. He made some adjustments at that time, which he believed had helped.

Over the next few days, Doug and I conversed several times over the phone and via email. He shared a bit about his life, and I learned just how lonely he was. And it was not hard to see why. I know very few people who can handle spending time with someone that intense.

Not only did I understand Doug's dilemma, I've been there myself. I spent the early part of my career struggling to harness my own intensity into the kind of passion that engages other people rather than scaring them away.

I have always been an enthusiastic person and assumed people appreciated that energy at all times. But after a networking function several years ago, one of my mentors asked me, "If you were hanging a picture on the wall, would you use a hammer or a sledge hammer?"

"A regular hammer, of course," I said.

"Think of your passion as a tool in your tool belt," she continued. "There are times when its use is critical, and there are times when using it will blow people away."

In essence, she taught me the importance of learning how to control my emotions, which isn't always easy. But understanding where my energy comes from helps me to use it effectively, without overwhelming people.

I shared this story with Doug and asked him, "What drives you?" While he didn't have a clear answer, the question gave him pause. When he figures out what's driving him (beyond his ego), he can begin to harness the intensity that makes him successful—without intimidating his team.

When you're clear about the deeper reason for your passion, your ego will release its grip and so will your intensity. Rather than seeking to become someone great, the greater good that you seek will bring you into your greatness.

I'll Have What He's Having

Unlike Doug, Jack Callahan knows what drives him, and that focused passion pulls others into his wake.

I met Jack in the professional recording studio that his parents built in their basement. I always knew Jack had a passion for music, but I never understood to what extent. My time in the recording studio was always with his father, Shaun. Jack would occasionally pop in to help with technical stuff, and I knew Jack had been the DJ for several events at his high school, but I had never seen him in action. That is, until I brought my friend Monalisa Arias over to meet the Callahans.

Monalisa is a talented musician with an extraordinary voice and an unbelievable ability to pick up just about any instrument and play it, beautifully. So it wasn't long before Monalisa, Jack, and Shaun started making random music together. Soon the jam session turned into a full-out dance fest, with Jack as DJ. His mom Sheila and I joined in, and the five of us danced for more than an hour...in the middle of the day!

Despite the fact I had talked up Monalisa and all the awards she's won for her vocal talents, Jack wasn't concerned a bit, nor was he trying to play what might please her. He just played the music he likes. His self-expression and confidence were stunning and infectious, making me wish I had a way to keep his energy with me.

The next time I saw Jack, I asked if he had a DJ business going. "My buddy and I do," he shared.

I asked if he had a logo, and he tossed me a hat with the design. "Do you have this logo on anything else?" I asked.

"Nope, we just have two hats."

"Can I get a shirt with your logo on it?"

"Sure," he said, clearly unsure how he would make that happen. The next time I saw him, he still didn't have shirts. So I tossed

$25 at him and told him to consider it his first order.

Why did I want a t-shirt with a high-school DJ's logo? Because I was inspired by his creative, expressive, confident energy, and I wanted to keep some of it with me.

It's the same reason so many people buy Monalisa's music on iTunes, along with many other bands. We identify with the words of the music; they're symbols that represent what we believe in.

Striking the Right Balance

What's the difference between Jack's and Doug's passions? Focus. Jack's passion was focused on his music, where Doug's was focused on preserving his image—with looking good enough, tough enough, and smart enough.

High intensity does not mean high passion, even though I confused the two at the networking function where my mentor told me to rein it in. At that time, I was still quite young and new to the business world. My intensity was deeply rooted in my passion to help young and seasoned professionals understand how to effectively communicate with one another. But my fear of not being smart or experienced enough clouded my ability to focus on what was really driving me.

When you're on fire about something that's not even about you, your passion becomes grounded, and other people have a chance to feed off that energy. Of course, before you can share your energy with others and inspire them the way Jack did for me, you must have enough of it to go around.

CHAPTER 26

Running on Fumes?

"It's not enough to be busy, so are the ants. The question is, what are we busy about?"

—Henry David Thoreau

Before you can think about creating the right kind of energy to move your team toward the finish line, you must have enough energy to get there yourself. Having a compelling vision doesn't count for much if you don't have the energy necessary to bring it to completion. If you're consistently stressed out and/or wiped out, you cannot expect your team to be vibrant and hard charging. Remember, they are mirroring you.

As a passionate, committed, leader, you'll always have plenty on your plate. You want to be successful—to do more, achieve more, go more places, talk to more people. You probably also have commitments in your personal life that require your time and energy.

Problem is, unless you're a robot or manage to clone yourself, there's only so much one person can do before running out of energy. So how do you accomplish everything that's important to you without losing stamina? For starters, get intentional about how you spend your time.

How to Clone Yourself

I recently attended a S.O.A.R. retreat—a three-day program that helps high-performing leaders and entrepreneurs "see, own, articulate, and release" their gifts and passions. During this phenomenal event, I met Charlotte, an entrepreneur who was struggling with this very issue.

Thirty minutes into the first day of our retreat, Charlotte arrived looking disheveled, exhausted, and annoyed. After being welcomed by the other seven participants and our host, Mali Phonpadith, Charlotte began telling us why she had chosen to participate in the retreat.

Being a mother, business owner, dermatologist, and wife, Charlotte was struggling to meet the demands of her full life. "Look at me. I'm fat and tired," she shared. "My staff keeps telling me I need to make some changes, because I'm clearly not looking the part. Some of my clients actually look me up and down when they walk into my office."

Now that's pressure!

Throughout the retreat, Charlotte remembered why she had chosen dermatology. Her face lit up as the other participants helped her identify the common themes she'd touched on throughout the retreat. "You're passionate about all-natural facial products," one participant pointed out. "And your heritage is Haitian. Why don't you start selling facial products made in Haiti?" Charlotte's hand ran across the page as she captured all the great ideas. Her spirit had clearly been reignited as she considered the bigger game she could play in her business and at home.

Yet while clarifying her vision and passion was a great start, Charlotte also needed help focusing her time. Just listening to her talk about her sleeping habits exhausted me: "I eat a big dinner around 2 a.m.," she said. "I go to bed for a couple of hours and then get up and have breakfast."

Yikes!

After everyone else had shared their ideas, I put three empty cups in front of Charlotte. Then I picked up a pitcher of water and said, "This is your energy for the day." I poured a little water into each cup and explained, "This is all the energy you get. Once it's gone, it's gone. Be intentional about where you're pouring your energy. You can do the things that are most important to you. You've just got to choose what those are, based on your greater vision and your personal priorities."

Then I added three more empty cups to the table, took one of the original cups (with water already in it), and poured a little bit into each empty cup.

"These empty cups are your team members," I explained.

"When you pour a little bit of your energy into their cups and empower them to help you, they can take some tasks off your plate. This frees you up to focus on what really matters to you—furthering your vision and spending time with your family, rather than getting bogged down in controlling each part of the process."

The truth is that to accomplish great things and live full lives, we all must make sacrifices. None of us has enough energy to do everything we want to do by ourselves. The trick is being intentional about what we're sacrificing and identifying people who can pick up some of our slack. Sacrificing is different from compromising. Do not compromise. It's important to command excellence, which means you have to pick the right teammates and put the ball fully in their court.

How to Say "No"

Charlotte is certainly not alone in her struggle to balance all the competing responsibilities in her life. There are super-achievers on Wall Street who are literally working themselves to death. It's become such an epidemic in the industry that three major banking institutions in New York have banned employees from the office for 36 hours each week (from 9 p.m. on Friday until 9 a.m. on Sunday).

It can be challenging to recognize when we're on the slippery slope of too much work and not enough play. It's even harder to intentionally take a step back. Having a team you can trust to help you get things done is a great way to protect your energy. Another is learning how (and when) to say no.

This is a personal struggle for me—not because I'm a pushover, but because I enjoy having new experiences and connecting with new people. So it's hard for me to turn down opportunities to do those things. But here's the thing: Energy is a renewable resource, not an unlimited one. Without making the time to rest and rejuvenate yourself, your battery will eventually run down...just like mine did a couple months ago.

Completely exhausted from nearly seven days of nonstop meetings, I wondered how in the world I was going to make it through the next two days. That's what you get for not saying no, I told myself, thinking that if I forced myself to stick to all my plans for the day, I would teach myself a valuable lesson about time management.

I immediately realized how unkind those words were and wondered how I could learn my lesson without beating myself up further. It was 4:30 a.m., and I had gotten very little sleep the previous night. My mind was racing, thinking about everything I needed to do. As I laid there, staring at the clock on my phone, I realized how tired I would be at my first meeting of the day.

You need to reschedule, I thought, as a wave of intense irritation came over me. Why didn't you manage your priorities better? The simple answer was that I wanted to do it all. Now here I was, for the second morning in a row, staring at my phone before sunrise.

I also had a radio interview scheduled that day, and I had already paid for an event I was really looking forward to attending that evening. The event hosts had even invited me to the after-party, and I had several guests attending.

I was wide awake and starting to feel sick. Clearly something had to give—either my sanity or my ego. So I rescheduled my appointment, reached out to my guests and the event hosts to wish them a delightful evening, and kept my promise for the 30-minute interview.

For some people, a heart attack or other major illness finally wakes them up to the consequences of their unhealthy decisions. For me, it was several nights of restless sleep after stretching myself way too thin.

Now I'm working to become more purposeful with each day—seemingly a life-long process. I do this by identifying the most important goal for the year that will catapult me closer to my vision. I also set three goals each for the year, the month, and the week. Before I agree to attend any meeting or event, I ask myself how doing so will help further my vision. It's not a perfect model, but it does give me a good guideline for deciding how to spend my time.

Work is important, but so are your health and happiness. When you focus on the most important outcomes you are committed to achieving, saying no becomes a great deal easier, because you know you're freeing yourself up to say yes to the right opportunities.

Clones are unnecessary. You can have your cake and eat it too. You simply need to know what kind of cake you want most.

Something's Gotta Give: Simple Steps to Reducing Your Workload

Small steps in the direction of your bigger goal are way better than giant, never-ending tasks that render you exhausted and unable to do anything well. Use the following questions to help you determine which tasks must happen now, and which aren't such a big deal in the grand scheme of your vision.

Step 1—Think Big Picture
What's the most important outcome you want in your career? What are you working hard to achieve, and why?

Step 2—Break It Down
What's the most important outcome you're committed to achieving this year in your career or business? What will be different as a result of achieving this goal?

Step 3—Now Break It Down Some More
What are the three most important tasks that need to be completed this month in order to achieve your long- and short-term goals?

Step 4—Call in Reinforcements
Who can help you complete the tasks you listed in

Step 3, or at the very least, help you make progress on them? If you're needed for any or all of it, ask yourself, "Why?" Then find a way to hand off responsibility, and give your team permission to make mistakes and learn.

Step 5: Dream Bigger, and Go Back to Step 1. Once you start down this path, you will free up your time to envision bigger opportunities for yourself and your team, and to start more projects that tap into your ever-increasing passion. Free yourself to dream bigger, and then find the right people to help make those dreams a reality.

For more on protecting your energy by focusing on what matters most to you, visit www.MeasurableGreatness.com/ HowToProvoke.

CHAPTER 27

Attack of the Energy Suckers

"There is no more powerful source of creative energy in the world than a turned-on, empowered human being. A conscious business energizes and empowers people and engages their best contribution in service of its noble higher purposes. By doing so, a business has a profoundly positive net impact on the world."
—John Mackey and Raj Sisodia, from *Conscious Capitalism*

Knowing what boosts and rejuvenates your energy is useful, but knowing what (or who) wastes it is just as important. Distractions abound in this fast-paced, technology-driven world, and they will steal your energy in a heartbeat if you let them.

Of course, not all distractions or time wasters can be avoided. Until we have Jetson-style flying cars, traffic is an inevitable part of life. And emergency situations happen all the time without our permission. But there are some distractions—both at work and home—that will continue to steal precious hours every single day, unless you make it a point to stop them.

4 Kinds of Energy Suckers

There are four categories of time wasters for most people: meetings, events, people, and activities. Some of these things can be welcome distractions and even productive parts of our days. Others just waste time and energy, and should be avoided.

Here's how to determine which is which:

- **Meetings**: In collaborative work environments, meetings can be super productive and even fun. But we've all sat through plenty of endless meetings that never needed to happen. A few best practices: Have a specific agenda and keep meetings to 30 minutes whenever possible.

- **Events**: Networking functions can be a great way to meet new people, build deeper connections, and begin relationships that could be hugely beneficial. They can also be the biggest waste of time, depending on whether you understand your purpose for being there.

- **Activities**: Most people waste a ton of time on email, social media, television, YouTube, and other unproductive tasks. Entertainment is great during your leisure time, but don't let it steal focus during work hours.

- **People**: Some people make our lives and work better and easier. Others only drain our energy. Identifying the people in your life who add to—and take away—your energy will help you make decisions about who to spend more/less time with, and who to hire.

To preserve your energy, know which meetings, events, activities, and people boost your energy, and which ones drain it. Then shift your schedule and the company you keep so you can spend most, if not all, of your time on productive, pleasurable experiences.

We all have different energy suckers to deal with, based on the type of work we do and how we structure our lives, but there are at least three universal time-wasters that drag most of us down: out-of-control email, social media distractions, and bad hires.

An Overloaded Inbox

The average worker spends 28 percent of his or her workweek managing email. The key to keeping all those communications under control is prioritizing. If your Inbox is keeping you from getting work done or having a life, then find a better system.

My friend Maimah was spending hours on email every day. She is a full-time contractor, a mother, and the founder and CEO of Tigerlily—a nonprofit organization dedicated to educating young women on breast cancer, so her time is precious. Yet she found herself staying up late into the night, responding to emails.

A couple years ago, I suggested she turn off the automatic "send/receive" feature on her email so she could focus on the activities that mattered most for her business and life, and check email if and when she had time.

"Won't people think I'm ignoring them if I don't respond to emails in a timely fashion?" she asked. "Then they might not want to support Tigerlily…or like me anymore."

"The people who want to support you will be there," I reminded her. "But you need to train them on how you handle emails, and when they can expect to hear back from you."

A few months ago, I sent Maimah an email. When a week had gone by with no response from her, I called to ask if she'd received my message. "I don't have time to look at my email anymore," she told me. "I'm busy doing the work that needs to get done. Don't you remember that conversation we had about email a couple years ago?"

Once Maimah realized she didn't need to respond to every email immediately, it stopped consuming her time. Now she can focus on what really matters to achieving her vision. "I have trained people how to treat me," she told me when I asked how this strategy was working for her. "Now that my employees and colleagues know they can't expect instant responses from me anymore, I can budget my time for emails, time for work, and time to breathe. My life is so much better now that I am no longer a slave to email!"

Take a cue from Maimah. You should control your Inbox, not the other way around. Train people to call with true emergencies. Otherwise you'll respond when you have time. It's as simple as that.

Being Too Social…Online

The average social networker spends 3.6 hours every day on social media (4.2 hours for those under age 35). And much of that is happening at work. In fact, 64 percent of employees visit non-work related websites each day, mostly social networks. That's a lot of wasted hours and energy, both at work and at home. Not that all time on social media is wasted. It can be a valuable tool for business and for connecting with friends and family. But it can also become a huge time-suck if you let it.

The trick to protecting your energy from social media distractions is clarifying your intentions—what outcomes you hope to get from the time investment. Social media serves two purposes for me: checking in with family, friends, and business associates, and marketing the products and services I've developed to help my customers.

The next step is to create a strategy that lets you work toward your social media goals, without spending so much time online that you get behind at work. I block off time for email and social media, collectively. When I check my emails, I respond to the quick ones immediately and place the thought-provoking ones to the side. If I get a message on social media, I steer the sender back to my email so I can keep track of all conversations in one place.

A fellow speaker and author, J.B. Glossinger, steers all questions to his Twitter account. He says, "This requires people to be succinct, which makes my life easier."

Maybe someday I'll switch to that model, but for now mine is working for me. That's the real goal: figuring out what works best for you and then adjusting your strategy based on the results you're getting.

Bad Hires

Many leaders simply focus on strengths, skills, and experience when hiring, and fail to consider a person's energy. Big mistake! Each employee's energy directly affects everyone else on the team.

D. Wayne Coffey, president and CEO of Coffey & Company, Inc., shared a story with me that proves this point well. Last year he hired a salesman who was referred by a head hunter. The candidate went through the company's rigorous hiring and onboarding process—which includes interviews with senior leaders, as well as a probationary period for the community to weigh in. During the probationary period, the entire team meets three times to discuss new hires and decide whether they're a good fit for the community—first after two weeks, and then again on the 30-day and 45-day marks.

During the 45-day review of this particular salesperson, Wayne was presented with a huge red flag. "One of my quietest employees said he made her feel uncomfortable and that he invaded her space," Wayne told me. "After she broke the ice, four other employees said the same thing. They noted that whenever they tried to step back and distance themselves, he would step forward. They used words like 'creepy' and 'negative energy.'"

After each of these team check-in meetings, Wayne's leadership team always follows up with the new employee to share the staff's concerns. "When I met with this guy, he was extremely defensive and stated they all were making things up," Wayne explained. "What I hoped he would say was, 'Oh my gosh, I'm so sorry. Let me make amends or change my behavior.' So I fired him the next morning, because I believe my job is to protect our culture."

The salesman went ballistic, cursing at Wayne and saying he could not fire him, which completely reaffirmed Wayne's decision to terminate. "The staff was shocked I would take this action," Wayne told me. "They knew I wanted a new salesperson and had paid a fee for finding him, but culture matters more."

Kudos to Wayne! Far too many leaders keep productive employees with bad attitudes or negative energy, thinking the money these folks bring into the company is worth the hit to corporate culture. It's not. Even one high-performing employee with a bad attitude sucks the energy (and productivity) out of everyone else on the team, bringing collective performance way down—not to mention making the office an unhappy place to work.

CHAPTER 28

Energy Trickles Down: A Tale of Two Airlines

"Your most unhappy customers are your greatest source for learning."
—Bill Gates

Your energy—and that of your team—doesn't just affect your employees. It also trickles down to your customers.

Most leaders know customer service is key to retaining a solid customer base. In fact, companies spend billions of dollars every year on customer service training and advertisements meant to show how customers are the first concern. Problem is, if front-line employees are unhappy, your customers will know it, and all that talk of customer-centricity will be meaningless. On the other hand, enthusiastic employees will do more for your brand than all the positive advertisements money can buy.

To illustrate my point, consider the following two stories—recent experiences I've had with major airlines.

Who Peed in Her Cheerios?

The day before Thanksgiving, I arrived at Chicago's O'Hare airport 30 minutes early, which meant I could potentially jump on an earlier flight. When I got to the gate, where I had hoped to board early, there was one employee at the XYZ Airlines counter. I asked how she was doing, and she responded, "Trying to keep up. There's just three of us here today...me, myself, and I." She was responsible for every customer and the flight crew, along with checking people in and ensuring everyone knew when to board.

As she was adjusting my ticket, a foreign gentleman approached her from the side with what he promised would be a quick question. "You're going to have to wait in line just like everyone else," she told him, pointing to me and the one other person behind me.

"It's no problem," I said, hoping to give way for his quick question.

"I don't know how they do it where you're from," she told him. "But we wait in line here!"

I felt bad for the guy. She was obviously under quite a bit of pressure. But I imagine he was too, considering it was the day before Thanksgiving and he was in a foreign country.

Later as my plane taxied out, they played the usual safety video, which I've heard a zillion times, so I started to tune out. That is, until I heard the lady in the video say, in a cheerful voice, "I've worked for XYZ Airlines for nearly 30 years."

Then a gentleman in the video said, "I've been with the company for more than 25 years."

The video closed with the tagline: "Customer service is a top priority for us here at XYZ Airlines." Then each "employee" repeated his or her own version of the same.

As I listened to them, I wondered how much it cost to produce that video. I also wondered what might happen to their customer service if they put those dollars toward "employee service"—like providing extra support for the lady at the ticket counter on one of the busiest travel days of the year. Then she would have more energy (and the right kind of energy) to put a happy, welcoming face on her company's brand.

When you're paying people to say nice things about your company, it's not very convincing, especially if you can't deliver what your advertisements promise. Rather than waste money trying to fool your customers, the better strategy is to take care of the people who actually interact with your customers—to do everything in your power to protect their energy so they can pass good vibes onto your customers.

Party in the Sky

Months after my experience with XYZ Airlines, I took a Southwest Airlines flight from San Diego, California, to Baltimore, Maryland. When I reached the gate, one thing was abundantly clear: This airline was different!

For one thing, the announcer had a smile on her face as she said into the microphone: "In preparation for boarding, please check your boarding group and number. We will begin by boarding group A, then B, and finally C. If you're in group A, please line up. Oh, and be sure to check with others to make sure you're in the right spot, based on your number."

I was in group A, but I had no idea where to stand, and the last thing I wanted to do was ask my fellow passengers. Fortunately one of them noticed my uncertainty and helped me find my spot in line.

As I boarded the plane, I couldn't help but notice the jovial spirit of the flight attendants, who were laughing and teasing each other playfully. The stewardess who gave the safety demonstration even had a little fun with us. She got our attention by saying, "I found this wallet on the airplane. Please let me know if it belongs to you." Everyone looked up immediately…just in time to see her giant smile. "That one gets 'em every time," she said.

Now that the team had our full attention, they did the demonstration, let us know what to expect throughout the flight, and got us prepared for takeoff.

When we were almost to Baltimore, another attendant asked us to return our seats to the upright position, fold up the tray tables, and turn off electronics. "Oh," she added, "and if the person next to you has headphones on, simply tap them on the shoulder and let them know what we're up to."

Within minutes the entire plane was ready to land, and the flight attendants never had to repeat themselves, leaving time for more fun. Just before we touched down, yet another flight attendant came on the microphone and shared a personal story about her first time in the U.S., a hilarious anecdote involving poison ivy.

I walked off that plane laughing, feeling good, and wanting all my future flights to be with Southwest Airlines. The company's clear commitment to employee happiness is leading to happy customers, and I want to be part of that.

While most companies want satisfied customers, few understand the connection between happy employees and happy customers. Instead most follow the old-school thinking: Take good care of the customer, and business will keep coming in. What they fail to realize is that serving customers means serving employees—using your VOICE to provoke their greatness.

HIGHLIGHTS
SECTION 5: ENERGY

1. Energy is contagious, so whatever vibes you're putting out there, your team is picking up—for better or for worse.

2. Before you can think about creating the right kind of energy to move your team toward the finish line, you must have enough energy to get there.

3. Nobody has enough energy to do everything they want to do by themselves. The trick is being intentional about priorities and picking the right team to pick up your slack.

4. Happy employees bring more to the team. They work harder, contribute more, build community, and pass their positive energy on to everyone around them.

5. There are four categories of time wasters for most people: meetings, events, people, and activities. Some of these things can be welcome distractions and even productive parts of our days. Others just waste time and energy, and should be avoided.

Your VOICE in Action

Opportunities to provoke are everywhere, not just at the office or in traditional leadership situations. Those who want to find and strengthen their VOICEs go beyond seeking opportunities to provoke; they open themselves up to being provoked.

Nearly 20 years after I bombed my lifeguard certification, I got the following text from my friend, Janice: "You should consider doing Swim Across America. I know you've been struggling with your hip. Maybe swimming will help? Once you sign up, you get free swim instruction for 15 weeks. Think about it."

I looked up Swim Across America (SAA) and learned it's a non-profit that raises money and awareness for cancer research, prevention, and treatment by hosting open water and pool swim events. It sounded good in theory, but as I contemplated Janice's suggestion, thoughts of drowning raced through my head. I was 19 years old when that swim instructor blew the whistle and instructed me to get out of the pool. Wanting badly to muscle my way through and get the certification that would secure me a cool summer job, I gasped for air as I asked, "Why are you kicking me out?"

"Because you look like you need to be saved," the instructor said without hesitation. Of course I needed to be saved; I had never practiced or even learned how to swim! Because I was an athlete and knew enough about swimming to keep my head above water, I'd figured I could wing it. Lesson learned!

Because Janice is both a friend and an avid swimmer, her text message kept stealing my attention. So I jumped online, took a peek at the website, and noticed the cost to sign up was just $25. With such a low entrance fee, there wasn't much to lose. If I really hated it, I could just stop. Then I noticed a line on the last page of the registration form: "By checking this box, I agree to raise a minimum of $500 before race day."

That's it, I thought. Clearly this isn't for me. I don't know how to swim, and I can't stand asking people for money.

Then I remembered Janice's suggestion that swimming might ease the pain in my left hip. The pain had gotten so bad that I'd had an MRI done and consulted three surgeons. It seemed I had two choices: reduce my exercise and hope it would go away, or get surgery and hope that would fix it. I didn't like either option.

Since I was joining a team, I figured my teammates would ensure we reached the team goal of $3,000. With that in mind, I completed the registration process, signed up for my first practice the very next day, and promptly put my promise to raise $500 out of my mind.

A Fish Out of Water

When I arrived for my first instruction, a very nice guy tossed me a swim cap. After listening to Annie, my first instructor, speak what sounded like gibberish, I turned to her and asked, "What do I do with this?"

"Seriously?" Annie asked.

"I don't know how to swim," I said flatly, hoping she could give me special attention in a class of 17 newbies.

"What do you know about swimming?" Annie asked.

Wanting to sound smart, but feeling like a complete idiot for getting myself into this, I said, "Gliding across the water."

"Wrong! Get in the pool," Annie commanded.

Twenty minutes later, having ingested several gallons of chlorinated water, I was saved by a thunderstorm. Learning the basics on the floor of a spin studio, which happened to be upstairs, was perfect for me. I listened closely and did every exercise she gave us in those remaining 40 minutes.

By week four, the water inhalation had tempered a bit, and I could swim 25 meters without stopping. I was so proud! I was also pretty embarrassed. I had learned the basics of swimming, but I hadn't raised a penny. I seriously considered just writing a check, but that wasn't what I'd committed to do. I had to face my other fear: asking for money. Rather than simply ask, I wrote and emailed about my experience, including why I had decided to learn to swim, and asked for contributions.

Two days later, I reached my goal. My $500 was raised, and so was my confidence. As I continued to practice that week, I felt the energy of every person who had contributed to my campaign. It was such a powerful experience that I decided to take the advice of my new friend Caroline and become a Wave Maker—the title given to those who raise $1,000.

During this time, my wife Yvette and I took a weekend away in Rehoboth, Delaware. While we were paddleboarding one day, Yvette suggested I swim across the bay. Rather than waste any time thinking about the dangers, I secured my paddleboard, grabbed my swim cap and goggles, and started swimming.

Yvette stayed to my right as I inhaled my fair share of salt water and stopped a million times before I made it to the other side. But before I could celebrate my victory, my hand swept across the scales of a giant fish.

"Big fish in the water," I said, with sincere panic in my voice. "Big fish!"

"Turn over onto your back," Yvette instructed. As soon as I did, I saw the concerned look on her face and realized there was very little she could do to help me from her paddleboard. I would need to calm myself down.

"It's OK, I'm OK," I started chanting.

Meanwhile Yvette poked her paddle into the water, only to realize the "fish" was just the bottom of the bay. I swiped my hand once more to confirm she was right. Of course she was, but that realization only instigated my next panic attack as I visualized the mud sucking me to the bottom.

Before I could work myself back into a frenzy, Yvette started paddling back to the other side and instructed me to follow her.

"Wait, just wait," I said. "I'm afraid of mud!" Then I dove to the bottom of the bay, scooped up a nasty chunk of it, brought it to the surface, and extended my arms toward Yvette. "Here," I said. "You can have my fear."

"That's gross, Misti," she said and paddled away.

I dropped the mud and proceeded to catch my first stride. I

swam the entire length of the bay (a little less than a mile) without stopping.

When I told this story to Caroline the following week at practice, she said, "If you can swim across the bay, you're going to be fine with the one-mile open water swim."

Having just made Wave Maker status, it occurred to me that I could up my own ante and set some new goals for myself: I would raise $3,000 and swim three miles in the open water. Having just learned how to swim, that goal seemed absurd. Perfect, I thought.

My hip was feeling better, I had formed new friendships, and I loved the idea of this challenge.

The Ripple Effect of VOICE

Three weeks before the swim, I reached my fundraising goal. Then I swam all three miles to complete the event.

Afterwards, as I sat on the beach of the Outer Banks in North Carolina, I thought about how Janice's VOICE had provoked me into doing the swim, and how my own VOICE had played a major role as well—growing in volume and passion throughout the process. Beyond simply learning how to swim, contributing to SAA, learning about the cancer research lab that benefits from the dollars raised, and cheering everyone else on, I had done all of this for myself, not for Janice. Her VOICE had simply created a foundation for me to strengthen my own.

Janice clearly had a vision for helping SAA, but she also saw an opportunity to help me. Having listened as I shared about the pain in my hip, the doctors I'd consulted, and the potential of an undesirable surgery, she had a compelling vision of a pain-free future for me. And she knew how to communicate her vision in the most powerful way—by making it meaningful to the person she wanted to provoke.

I can only imagine how I might have responded to Janice's text had she said, "You should come help me raise money for cancer research," and included nothing about my hip. I don't think I would have signed up, and I certainly wouldn't have made it past the 12th gallon of inhaled chlorinated water before I opted out of the swim and just wrote a check to support the cause.

Janice took ownership for provoking me by showing up several times to coach me—both at my community pool and during my official practice sessions. Her text message was a clear statement of her intention to help me, and SAA. Having been a part of this swim community for years, her connections to the people involved only fueled her energy to recruit others who could benefit.

Had it not been for Janice's VOICE, it's unlikely I would have addressed my fears of drowning, asking for money, big fish, mud, or sharks. By focusing on the very thing I wanted, Janice provoked me…right into contributing to a worthy cause, learning how to swim, and inspiring dozens of others by the sheer act of taking action toward a goal that was important to me.

The greatest part? My VOICE strengthened as a result of learning how to swim. I took her vision—for me and SAA to have a healthier future—and ran with it, adjusting along the way. I took ownership of the promise I made, overcame my fears, and raised the funds. Then I turned around and got intentional all over again about raising even more money. The sense of connection I got as a result of swimming with my new community every week furthered my resolve to push harder and contribute more. And every time I reached a new milestone, even during practice, my energy level increased, fueling my passion to stretch myself even further.

Raising $1,000 inspired me to take on Yvette's challenge of swimming across the bay, which further inspired me to set new goals. Overcoming a handful of fears fueled my efforts in every other part of my life, which led me to unintentionally inspire (and energize) countless others by sharing my journey.

That's the beautiful thing about provoking: When you do it, your VOICE creates a ripple effect, inspiring not only your team, but also their teams and communities, your customers, and the world.

So what are you waiting for? Find your VOICE and start provoking greatness.

Acknowledgements

Provoking Greatness started off as a book about stubborn leadership. Then it switched to a book about focus, but somehow I couldn't seem to focus on it! Nearly three years later, it has blossomed into a book about the art of provocation.

While many editors would have wiped their hands clean of such chaos, Taylor Mallory Holland encouraged and supported me along the way, and helped bring this book to life.

Although we certainly enjoyed good laughs about not being able to focus on a book about focus, this book would not have come to be without the relentless support of my wife, Yvette Nash. Thank you, my love, for always reminding me of the gifts I have to offer.

Thank you, Mali Phonpadith, for your spiritual guidance and savvy messaging suggestions. And to Rob Barbour—who jumped in, reviewed my book, and provided excellent marketing suggestions.

Wendy Wolock, you are the biggest cheerleader I've ever met, and I'm forever grateful for your love of the courageous spirit.

Thank you, LN Lurie, for jumping into this journey at just the right time, sharing your gift of audio engineering, and always helping me see where I naturally teach.

A big "thank you" to the Callahans—Shelia, Shaun, and Jack—who not only stirred creative ideas, but also shared dozens of relatable/helpful stories, listened to my fears, and let me use their professional recording studio to create the audio version of this book. Thank you for the laughs, games, and dancing. You bring so much joy to this planet!

I am eternally grateful to my reviewers, who took time out of their schedules to review this book and provide candid/helpful feedback. Thank you, Tim Overstreet, Renee Wynn, Janie Tiedeman, Mike Lombardi, Kevin Bonner, Rob Barbour, and Elaine Susel.

The foundation and structure of Provoking Greatness was inspired by one of the most creative left-brained people I know. Art Jacoby, what a gift you are! If not for your guidance, the structure and clarity of the VOICE model might never have come to be.

Greg Conderacci, if it wasn't for your provoking words—"Show me how to intentionally spark greatness in another"—I would never have considered researching the science behind the art of provocation. Thank you for provoking me!

A very special "thank you" to my sister, Carolyn Franke, who always reads my writing and supports my journey. Carolyn, this simple act means more than you'll ever know.

CPSIA information can be obtained at www.ICGtesting.com
Printed in the USA
BVOW02*0058170615

403487BV00004B/2/P